THE BLESSINGS OF BROKENNESS

Books by Dr. Charles F. Stanley

A Touch of His Freedom
A Touch of His Love
A Touch of His Peace
A Touch of His Wisdom

THE BLESSINGS OF BROKENNESS

WHY GOD ALLOWS US
TO GO THROUGH HARD TIMES

CHARLES STANLEY

ZondervanPublishingHouse
Grand Rapids, Michigan

A Division of HarperCollins*Publishers*

To the members of First Baptist Church of Atlanta,
who faithfully supported me in my times of brokenness.

CONTENTS

CONTENTS

Chapter One

BROKEN AND BLESSED?

$\mathcal{B}$roken.

Blessed.

The two words don't seem to go together. If anything, they seem to be exact opposites.

We all know what it means to be broken—to be shattered, to feel as if our entire world has fallen apart, or perhaps been blown apart. We all have times in our lives when we don't want to raise our heads off the pillow, and when we feel certain the tears will never stop flowing. Brokenness is often accompanied by emptiness—a void that cannot be filled, a sorrow that cannot be comforted, a wound for which there is no balm.

Nothing *feels* blessed about being broken. The most painful and difficult times of my life have been those times when I felt broken. I don't like pain, suffering, or feelings of brokenness any more than anybody else does. Certain circumstances in life *hurt*, at times so intensely that we think we will never heal.

One of the things I have discovered through being broken, however, is that *after* brokenness we can experience God's greatest blessings. After brokenness our lives can be the most fruitful and have the most purpose. The dawn after a very dark and storm-wreaked night is glorious. Feeling joy again after a period of intense mourning can be ecstatic. A blessing can come in the wake of being broken.

But this blessing comes only if we experience brokenness fully and confront *why* it is that God has allowed us to be broken. If we allow God to do his complete work in us, blessing will follow brokenness.

RUNNING FROM OR FACING THE PAIN?

Most people do not understand what the Bible teaches about brokenness; therefore, the last thing they want in life is to experience it. Rather, they spare no effort in running from brokenness.

In a time when we hear so much talk about prosperity, about God's healing our illness, about God's desiring our happiness, the message of brokenness does not appeal to many people. In fact, it only appeals to those who want God's best!

Why do I say that?

Because God is in the process of changing what we desire, far more than he is in the process of giving us what we desire. God is refining us, fashioning us, and making us into the people with whom he wants to live forever.

God didn't create us to give us our every whim and wish, but rather, to bring us to the position where we will want to do whatever God desires. He created us for himself.

If I asked you, "Do you really want God's best for your life?" I feel confident that you would say, "Yes, of course!"

If I asked you, "Do you truly want to become who God predesigned you to become before you were born?" you would probably say, "Absolutely!"

If I asked you, "Are you willing for God to do anything necessary to bring you to total surrender so that he is free to accomplish all that he wants to do for you and all he wants to make out of you?" I wonder what your response might be.

To have God's very best, we must be willing to submit our all to him, so that God's Holy Spirit so compellingly and overwhelmingly guides us that we are living, walking expressions of the Lord Jesus Christ on the earth today.

This state does not come easily. Even when we yield ourselves fully and completely to God, we are still being refined. Refinement occurs over time and through a myriad of circumstances and situations. No person arrives "fully formed" as a mature Christian the instant he or she accepts Christ Jesus as Savior. We become new creatures spiritually, but we must grow up into the nature of Christ. Growth is a process—one that includes setbacks, failures, hard lessons, and yes, brokenness. Our growth includes not only a spiritual growth, but a renewal of our minds and emotions.

Old habits are not easily changed. Old desires cling to us in spite of our efforts to remove them from our hearts and minds. Old patterns of responding die hard. In many cases, old relationships must be renewed or redefined. Sometimes others whom we love dearly don't seem to grow spiritually as fast as we might desire, or as quickly as we ourselves grow.

Even in our most pliable and compliant state, we also suffer from never fully knowing our own selves and, therefore, never fully knowing the extent of our own sin. In many ways, we do not see our own dark side. We may *think* we have repented of every sin, only to have God reveal to us yet another area of our life that needs to be subjected to his forgiving love, cleansed, and then changed, healed, or renewed by the power of the Holy Spirit.

Again and again, we find ourselves being broken in order that our old nature might be chipped away, a rough spot in our character might be sanded, or an unknown talent might be revealed.

The process is painful and difficult.

Nevertheless, it is good.

Brokenness is not something to be shunned or avoided at all cost. Rather, it is something to be faced with faith. If we truly want to be all that God designed us to be, and therefore all that God desires for us to be, we must submit to him during times of brokenness and allow him to reveal to us *why* we are going through what it is we are experiencing and *what* he desires for us to learn from the situation.

A PERFECT VESSEL

One day the Lord spoke to the prophet Jeremiah:

"Go down to the potter's house, and there I will give you my message." So I went down to the potter's house, and I saw him working at the wheel. But the pot he was shaping from the clay was marred in his hands; so the potter formed it into another pot, shaping it as seemed best to him.

Then the word of the LORD came to me . . . "Can I not do with you as this potter does? . . . Like clay in the hand of the potter, so are you in my hand." (Jeremiah 18:2–6)

Have you ever seen a potter at work on a potter's wheel? A vessel takes shape as the potter's hands mold and guide the upward flow of clay. But then, if the vessel does not meet with the potter's approval—perhaps because of a flaw in the design or a bubble in the clay—the clay is smashed down again onto the wheel, and the clay is reshaped. The potter's purpose is not to destroy his work, but rather, to make a more perfect work—to shape and fashion something more beautiful and more functional.

In like fashion, God is at work in our lives, shaping and making us into the people he longs for us to be so that we might bring glory to him and be of maximum use to him in the building of his kingdom.

Which would you rather be? A vessel of your own design, based upon your finite mind and limited creativity, power, and wisdom—a vessel of limited use and passing value? Or a vessel of his design, based upon his infinite wisdom, love, and power—a vessel of unlimited use and eternal, unmeasured value?

In choosing to be fashioned by God, we inevitably must choose to yield to brokenness and to allow God to remake us and renew us as he desires—even if that means suffering pain, hardship, and trials.

Brokenness can be a path toward great blessing, but only when we allow God to do the breaking and to design the blessing.

Chapter Two

GOD WANTS
THE BEST FOR US

So often when tragedies strike or hard times engulf us, we ask, "Where's God?"

In asking this question, we make an assumption that God must not have known what was about to befall us or else he would have prevented it. Or we assume that God must not love us, because surely, if he loved us, he would keep us from all hurtful times and hard experiences.

Both assumptions are wrong.

The fact is, God knows. And God loves.

CONSIDER MY SERVANT

When we experience difficult times or feel great inner pain and turmoil, we usually try to assign blame. We say one of two things: either "The devil caused this" or "God caused this."

The greater likelihood is this: The devil caused it, and God allowed it.

Consider the story of Job.

Job was a man whom the Bible describes as being "blameless and upright; he feared God and shunned evil" (Job 1:1). Satan came before the Lord, and the Lord asked him, "Have you considered my servant Job? There is no one on earth like him" (Job 1:8).

Satan replied, "Does Job fear God for nothing? ... Have you not put a hedge around him and his household and everything he has? You have blessed the work of his hands, so that his flocks and herds are spread throughout the land" (Job 1:9–10).

God subsequently gave Satan permission to touch Job's possessions, but not Job's body. Satan moved against Job, and Job's sons and daughters, as well as all his flocks and herds and servants died. Job said, "Naked I came from my mother's womb, and naked I will depart. The LORD gave and the LORD has taken away; may the name of the LORD be praised" (Job 1:21). Job did not blame God for these tragedies.

Satan again came before God, and God said, "Have you considered my servant Job? ... He still maintains his integrity" (Job 2:3).

Satan said, "A man will give all he has for his own life. But stretch out your hand and strike his flesh and bones, and he will surely curse you to your face" (Job 2:4–5). The Lord then allowed Satan to afflict Job, but required that he spare his life. Satan caused painful sores to erupt on Job's body, from his feet to the top of his head. Job plunged into great misery.

Job's wife attempted to convince Job to curse God and die. His friends tormented him with various accusations. In the end, Job said to God, "I know that you can do all things; no plan of yours can be thwarted" (Job 42:2).

God surely knew that Job was being afflicted. He allowed it to happen for reasons that were his alone. Throughout Job's pain and losses, God never abandoned Job for even a moment. He knew at each step of the way how Job was being afflicted. God also knew how he was refining Job.

The good news for us anytime we find ourselves being broken is this: God sees the beginning and the end of our lives. He has a good future designed for us—one we may not experience fully on this earth.

In Job's case, when Job prayed for his friends and declared that he had no questions of God, but rather, that he realized he was the one whom God had the privilege to question—a position of total surrender—the Lord made Job to prosper again. He gave Job twice as much as he had before—greater flocks, more children, and the comfort and consolation of his brothers and sisters and everyone who knew him. He lived in health to an old age.

Whatever it is that we may experience and however we may be broken, God has a good end for us, too. Our period of brokenness is not the end, but rather, a passage and a process to a new beginning that is even more glorious.

Yes, God knows. And God loves.

God Always Acts Out of Love

The motivation behind everything that God does in our lives and everything he allows in our lives is love.

God does not allow brokenness in our lives because he is ruthless, cruel, heartless, or without compassion. No! To the contrary. God sees the full potential for our lives, and he deeply desires an intimate, loving spiritual relationship with us. He wants to bring about our best, and for us to experience him in the fullness of his love, wisdom, power, strength, and goodness. He allows brokenness in our lives *in order to bring about* a blessing.

God never breaks us in anger or wrath. Rather, God moves in on our lives because he loves us too much to see us continue in our sin, remain in a lukewarm spiritual state, or go unfulfilled in his purposes for our lives. God loves us too much to see us remain as we are. His love motivates him to act so that we might change, grow, and become spiritually mature and whole in spirit, mind, and body. God loves us so much that he wants to have close intimate spiritual fellowship with us—something he cannot have as long as we are in rebellion or resistance against him. He longs to strip sin from our lives. He longs to use us in a holy and effective service of supernatural ministry.

God's love compels him to discipline and chastise us so that we might be refined for his purposes on this earth.

CHASTISEMENT VERSUS PUNISHMENT

Punishment is often confused with brokenness. We must be very clear on this point: Chastisement and punishment are two different things.

Punishment is for unbelievers only. It is an expression of God's wrath against those who have rejected the only Sin-bearer who can separate a sinful person from God's wrath.

God's holiness and purity compel him to move swiftly against sin wherever and in whomever God finds it—just as bright light rushes in to overcome a dark room. God cannot tolerate sin. He must eradicate it from his presence.

The unbeliever is one who has rejected the blood of Jesus Christ, denied the sacrifice that Christ made on the cross, and therefore has no barrier between his sin and God's holiness. The unbeliever is in an awesome, terrible position—totally exposed to God's wrath.

Chastisement is God's method of disciplining the believer. God's purpose is to lead a believer to confront, remove, or change those habits, attitudes, and beliefs that keep the believer from growing into the full stature of Christ's likeness. Chastisement is a *training tool* that God uses in making us whole and spiritually mature. It is God's method for preparing us for a supernatural ministry of service under the direction of the Holy Spirit.

Punishment flows from God's wrath. The end result is eradication, elimination, and total estrangement from God. For example, God punished the followers of Korah for treating him with utter contempt. The earth split apart and swallowed them, with their households, as a sign to the Israelites. (See Numbers 16.)

Chastisement flows from God's love. The end result is change, growth, and development. For example, God allowed Miriam to be struck with leprosy and then restored as a lesson to teach her that her criticism of Moses was an error. (See Numbers 12.)

God loves us so much that he longs for us to reflect his very nature and literally to *be* the body of Christ on the earth today. Chastisement is a means of refinement—just as the dross and impurities are removed from metal, so God strips us of sin and faults that keep us from being made whole. The prophets repeatedly likened the refining purpose of God's love to that of a refiner and purifier of silver and gold (Isaiah 48:10; Malachi 3:3; Zechariah 13:9).

GOD DOES NOT WANT TO BREAK OUR SPIRIT

God's purpose is *not* to break our spirit. The person with a broken spirit is not whole or growing toward spiritual maturity. God can't entrust his supernatural ministry to a person with a broken spirit.

No, God's purpose is not to break our spirits, but rather, to break the stubbornness of our wills. He does this so he might effect his will in our lives. His will is always for our good, for our blessing.

Every parent knows that children are born with a me-first, egocentric stubbornness. "Mine!" and "No!" seem to be two of the first words every child learns and uses freely. Both are rooted squarely in a child's egocentric pride and desire to govern his or her own life.

A good parent knows that this streak of stubbornness and pride must be broken if a child is going to be obedient—not only to the parent, but to all authority, including the authority of God. The breaking of a child's stubbornness is not done to break the child's spirit, but rather, to help the child grow up to be a useful, productive, law-abiding, generous, and loving spouse, friend, parent, citizen, and member of the body of Christ.

A child who is allowed to remain stubborn and proud will become an adult who is despicable to be around, who is ill-tempered, who is sometimes pathologically criminal, and who has very little capacity to receive or give love. A child who is allowed to remain stubborn and proud becomes an adult who has little ability to feel joy, hope, or satisfaction.

Just as a parent breaks a child's stubborn pride and willful disobedience, so God seeks to break within us the pride and disobedience that keeps us from being the loving, generous, Christlike people he believes we can be.

GOD DOES NOT DELIGHT IN CAUSING US PAIN

Just as it is not God's desire to break our spirit, neither is it God's purpose to cause us pain. Are pain and suffering the end result of what God desires for us? No! God may allow or bring about circumstances and situations in our lives that seem painful to us, but these circumstances and situations are *tools* that God uses to bring us to a position where we are willing to surrender our lives completely to him.

Our next question should then be, Is a Christian ever a victim? Yes, sometimes. As Christians, we are victims only to the extent that others have injured us physically or hurt us emotionally. But we must recognize that God has allowed these painful experiences in our lives for some reason.

When we see ourselves as victims, we live in the past and wallow in our pain. If we see ourselves as beloved by a God who is preparing us for a special future and service, which he alone may know, then we find strength to endure the past pain and move forward.

God is sovereign. He can stop anything he desires to stop. He will not override human will, however. If people close to us open themselves to evil, we may suffer in the wake of their evildoing. For example, if a man becomes an alcoholic, his wife and children may suffer from his rage or neglect. God knows this. He loves us, however, and has the ability to redeem these situations in our lives for good.

As a child, I suffered many things that I would consider to be injustices or abuse. My father died when I was only nine months old, and I spent much of my early childhood alone while my mother worked. Later in my childhood, my mother married a man who was very abusive to me and to my mother, not only emotionally but physically. Even so, I have never once felt myself to be a victim. Rather, I choose to believe that I am a beloved child of God. God is up to something in my life that is ultimately for my good. He has a purpose in allowing bad things to happen, and his purpose extends not only to my life alone, but to the lives of others whom I may influence or help.

If we believe Romans 8:28 to be true, we must believe it to be true for *all* circumstances in our lives: "We know that in all things God works for the good of those who love him, who have been called according to his purpose."

We must never limit God's ability to turn even the worst, most vile experience in our lives into something productive, beneficial, and positive. When I look back on my childhood, I can see how God has used my experiences with loneliness, pain, and insecurity to help me to minister more effectively to people today who are lonely, hurting, and insecure. I have a strong message for them: "If God could bring me through, he can bring you through. If God could heal my hurts and make me whole, he can heal your hurts and make you whole." Those experiences of my early childhood made me tougher in some ways to cope with life's struggles, and they made me tender in other ways to feel more compassion for people who are struggling. While I hurt at the time, and while the memory of those experiences may be painful, I also am able to count my early experiences as a blessing to my life. They were hard lessons that resulted in good for me and for others.

A young man recently wrote to In Touch Ministries after his release from prison. He had been convicted of a drug-related crime he committed as a teenager. Not only did this man experience a spiritual renewal while in prison, but he now uses his past experience to speak to teenagers about the dangers of yielding to peer pressure, and especially to the use of drugs. He doesn't blame his parents, his neighborhood, or his impoverished conditions for his behavior in the past. Rather, he accepts personal responsibility for his actions and is seeking to find a way to help others. He wrote, "I can see how God had a plan all along. He didn't abandon me when I got into drugs and crime. God allowed me to be arrested and convicted. If he hadn't, I'd probably have died on the streets a long time ago. He kept his hand on me all the way through prison. He brought someone into my life who would share Christ with me. He led me to a church after I got out of prison, and then he led me to an opportunity to tell others about Christ and about how to stand up to the pressures that teenagers feel."

Regardless of the source of our pain, we must accept that God knows, God loves, and God is at work. We may not be responsible for what has happened to us, but we are responsible for our response to it. We must ask ourselves, "How can I walk through this pain? How can I benefit or profit spiritually from this?"

A man once came to me and said, "I have been dating a woman, and I'm starting to like her a lot. She said to me just this last week, 'I've been date-raped. There's a lot you need to know about me before we get any closer.'"

I said to him, "Before you get into this relationship any deeper, you need to help this woman get into Christian counseling so she can learn how to deal with this situation in her past. Otherwise, you are going to find yourself in a situation you won't be able to handle."

He took my advice. This woman went through a very difficult time letting go of her victim identity. To a certain extent, she had given in to being a victim, and she had even begun to enjoy the sympathy she got from other people because of what had happened to her. As a result, she lived her life in the past. Her past overshadowed both her present and her future. Her date-rape experience began to define her identity.

If any experience in your past is defining you today—*other* than your salvation experience—then you have serious work to do. You very likely are still allowing yourself to be victimized, rather than allowing yourself to be redeemed and healed by the love of God. As long as we see ourselves as victims, we are not able to embrace the wholeness God has for us.

Finally, this woman was able to say, "I've got to move ahead in my life. I've got to find a way to work through this experience with God's help so I can be a whole person again."

DO YOU REALLY KNOW WHAT'S HAPPENING?

Perhaps far more revealing and helpful than the questions, "Does God know what's happening to me?" or "Does God care about the pain I'm feeling?" are these questions we each need to ask ourselves:

- Do *I* know what is happening to me?
- Do *I* care about what God desires to do in my life?

God knows what he is about in your life, but do you know what God is about in your life? Do you have an awareness of what God is doing?

Sometimes that awareness comes later, with a little clearer perspective on the past. When I look back in my life, I can see clearly how God has changed me. I've been broken, shattered, beaten, smashed, pruned, and chiseled on, and I didn't like the feeling of brokenness any more than you do. But I can tell you this—I thank God for what he's done. Every chisel blow, every hammer blow, every cut of the knife, every slice into my innermost being, every tear, every pain, every hurt, every disappointment, every disillusionment, every moment of despair has been worth it all just to know in my heart that God has my all.

Ask God to reveal to you what he is doing in your life—and what he desires to do for you, in you, and through you—as the result of your brokenness.

Put your brokenness into the perspective of God's greater work in you.

If I were to ask you, "What is it that you are holding onto that you would be willing to keep holding onto
even if it meant missing God's best for you through all
eternity?" I doubt if you would be able to give me an
answer. Nothing in this temporal world is worth grasping
or clinging to in exchange for God's best through all eternity. Nothing holds the value of God's great design for
your life!

Chapter Three

WHY WE
ARE BROKEN

A young man once said to me, "I've been a Christian for two years, Pastor, and I can't begin to tell you how different my life is now. Last week I went to a prayer meeting on a Friday night, and I thought to myself, *Man, if anybody had told me two years ago that I'd be going to a prayer meeting on a Friday night and praising God and singing songs about God and liking every minute of it, I would have said, 'You're nuts!'*"

Then he added in a very serious, thoughtful tone, "Sometimes I wonder, though, why I had to go through such awful experiences before I came to the Lord. I was an alcoholic. I used people and loved things, rather than loving people and using things. I got into trouble with the law and came very close to killing a couple of people because I had an accident while driving under the influence. I wish God had saved me a whole lot sooner."

I said to him, "Perhaps something in you had to die before you could fully live."

He thought about that for a moment. "Yeah, you're right. I wasn't ready to give up what I called the 'good life' until about two and a half years ago. I thought I had a great life until that time. It's only now that I know what a terrible life I was leading."

Before any of us can fully live as God has created us to live, we first must die to our desire to control our own lives or to live life according to our plan and will.

SOMETHING HAS TO DIE FOR LIFE TO BEGIN

One important passage of Scripture on brokenness is John 12:24–25. In preparing his disciples for his crucifixion and resurrection, Jesus said: "I tell you the truth, unless a kernel of wheat falls to the ground and dies, it remains only a single seed. But if it dies, it produces many seeds" (John 12:24).

As long as you hold a kernel of grain in your hand, you have only one grain. You can place it on the barn floor, put it on a windowsill, or even place it under a glass dome and keep it forever, but it will still be only one grain. Nothing will come of it or from it. Eventually, it will rot and turn to dust.

Once you take that seed, however, and drop it into the earth and cover it up with soil, you have positioned it to die—but this time with the purpose of reproducing life. The elements in the soil, the heat of the sun, and the moisture in the earth will all work on the outer shell of that seed. Before long, the outer shell breaks, and a little green sprout begins to push its way up through the soil until eventually it breaks through into the sunshine. A root begins to grow downward, anchoring the seedling to the soil. The seed itself disappears as a stalk of grain grows and eventually produces an ear of corn or a head of wheat. That ear of corn or head of wheat holds dozens of grains, each of which has the capacity to grow into a plant of its own.

From one grain of wheat, a person could eventually plant a million acres of wheat, if all he did was replant all of the fruit of one grain, and then all the fruit from its grains, and so forth.

Jesus was teaching that as long as the grain remains alone—unplanted and unyielded—it cannot bear fruit. He was describing, of course, what was about to happen to him. As long as Jesus remained alive, a few people might be healed, a few might benefit from his miracles, a few might turn to God by his teaching and preaching, but ultimately, the world would remain unforgiven.

Before his life could be extended and multiplied, Jesus had to die. Once he had died and risen again, his life could be multiplied millions of times, just as it has been down through the centuries. Those of us who have accepted him as our Savior and have been forgiven of our sins had our names written in the Lamb's Book of Life *because he was willing to die.*

In turn, he calls upon each of us to take up our cross—sacrificially dying to ourselves and giving ourselves to his cause—in order that we might live for him and according to his purposes.

Jesus went on to say, "The man who loves his life will lose it, while the man who hates his life in this world will keep it for eternal life" (John 12:25).

We must be willing to die to our affections, dreams, desires, ambitions, and goals, and then be totally willing for the Lord Jesus Christ to have his way in our lives. Only then can we truly know life to the fullest and find our purpose in life realized completely. We must die to self in order to become more of ourselves and eternally ourselves!

We must break ourselves of our intense love of self if we are ever to allow God's love to envelop us and fill us.

Several other passages of Scripture echo this same teaching: In holding on to our own desires and our own will, we lose. In letting go and letting God have control, we win. (See Matthew 10:39 and Matthew 16:24–26.)

You may be asking, "But why does God require that something be put to death in order for it to be made alive?" The fullness of God's reasons are known only to God. But we can see that this principle holds true throughout his creation.

We have the juice of grapes only because somebody has crushed the grapes. We have bread only because somebody has crushed the grain into flour. We have fully productive and useful lives only because God has crushed our self-will.

GOD WANTS TO DESIGN OUR FUTURE

I have discovered through the years that those who are young sometimes have a more difficult time submitting their lives completely to the Lord. They see the future stretched out before them, filled with what they perceive to be unlimited opportunities. Satan tricks them into thinking that the future cannot be good without this relationship, or the fulfillment of that sexual desire, or the pursuit of this vocational commitment, or the acquisition of that particular possession. They begin to pursue what Satan holds out as the "ideal way to live." His plan, of course, never includes God.

The result of pursuing what Satan holds out as desirable is a spirit of *striving*. Striving is hard work—it depends solely on what an individual person is capable of doing (or of convincing others to do). Striving has an element of greed to it—there's always more to be achieved, earned, or acquired. Striving has self at its core—it wants what it wants. When a person is striving for something, she has little regard for harm that may be done to others, or even to her own body or soul. Striving is raw ambition. And ultimately, striving is bondage.

The illusions that Satan holds out as being objects that give value, meaning, and worth to one's life are just that—illusions. They are like a mirage in the desert. You can struggle and scrape and claw and crawl toward that mirage with all of your energy, year after year, and never arrive. What appears to be life-giving is actually dry dust.

Is it wrong to like quality things or to purchase the best you are able to afford? Is it wrong to desire a spouse and children? Is it wrong to want to succeed in your work?

No! What is wrong is when we feel we can't live without those things. What is wrong is substituting the acquisition of things, relationships, and accomplishments for a relationship with God. When we set our eyes on the accomplishment of *our* goals, we nearly always lose sight of God's goals for us. Only when we make our relationship with God our number-one priority can God bring us into a position where we can achieve and receive what will truly satisfy us.

I once counseled a young man who was very upset at a breakup with his girlfriend. He had fallen deeply in love with this young woman and had anticipated spending the rest of his life with her. When she jilted him for another guy, he was badly wounded.

As we talked, he admitted to me that he had begun to plan his entire life around what his girlfriend desired—he had moved to be closer to her, he took a job that she thought was good for him, he began to attend her church, he dressed in the way she desired. In addition, he felt a great deal of pressure from her to be successful financially.

I asked him, "Did God tell you to make this move or accept this job?" He confessed that he hadn't even asked God about any of these changes he had made in his life. I encouraged him to start at that point in his recovery from a broken heart. "Ask God what *he* desires for you to be and do," I said.

I didn't see this young man again for several years. By the time we met again, he was married to a lovely young woman and they had a six-month-old son. He said to me, "Things really changed, Pastor Stanley, after I started doing things God's way. I moved back to my hometown and took a job that the Lord opened up for me. I met my wife at the church where I had grown up. She and her family had moved to town while I was at college. The Lord really brought our lives together in a way that we knew it was God's planning. We have the same goals in life."

All of the things Satan holds out as not only desirable but *necessary* for our identity in the future are deceptions. His intent is not to see a person blessed, but rather, to bring about a person's doom. If there's anything in our lives that we think we just can't live without, that should be a warning sign to us to reevaluate our relationship with God and to take another look at our priorities.

Jesus clearly taught, "Do not worry, saying, 'What shall we eat?' or 'What shall we drink?' or 'What shall we wear?' For the pagans run after all these things, and your heavenly Father knows that you need them. But seek first his kingdom and his righteousness, and all these things will be given to you as well" (Matthew 6:31–33).

God knows what you need. He knows what is best for you—including in what quantity. The fact is, we can live with very little, but we can never truly live without God. He is what we need first, foremost, and always. He is the only one whom we truly can't do without!

The things that Satan holds out to us as "must haves" for the future are passing, temporal things. If we are willing to give up striving for these things and seeking after them no matter the cost, and instead, turn to God, he will satisfy all of our longings for the future with perfect fulfillment. If we are willing to give up defining our own future, he'll give us something better than we could ever arrange, manipulate, or create. His best will be ours—but only if we are willing to die to our selfish independent streak and to submit our lives completely to him.

GOD WANTS TO SET OUR GOALS

A young woman asked me after she had heard me preach about this, "Pastor, is it wrong to set goals? It seems to me that you are saying that we should just live day to day, trusting God, and not have any plans or goals."

It's not wrong for us to set goals—what's wrong is when we set goals apart from asking God what his goals for us might be. We must always approach our goal setting with earnest prayer, asking, "What is it, God, that you desire for me to do and say and be?"

Our prayer must be the same as the one that Jesus prayed in the Garden of Gethsemane, "Not as I will, but as you will" (Matthew 26:39).

WE ARE CHRIST'S WORKMANSHIP

Who is responsible for your accomplishments and success in life?

Do you consider that *you* are responsible for who you will become and what you will succeed in doing? Or are you relying on God to live his life through you and to change you so that he might use you for his purposes?

These are two very different perspectives. We rarely yield quickly or easily to brokenness if we believe that we hold our destiny in our own hands.

The wise person faces the reality that God both deserves and demands the right to everything that we are. He has the authority and right to express his life through us—through our lips, eyes, hands, feet, body, thoughts, emotions—in any way he so chooses. We are not merely to be reflections of the way Christ was, but we are to be living, walking expressions of the life of Christ in the world today.

The Bible tells us that once we have accepted Jesus Christ as Savior, we do not own ourselves and we do not govern or determine our own future. Paul wrote, "For it is by grace you have been saved, through faith—and this not from yourselves, it is the gift of God—not by works, so that no one can boast. For we are God's workmanship, created in Christ Jesus to do good works, which God prepared in advance for us to do" (Ephesians 2:8–10).

Just as you didn't earn your salvation, so you are not responsible for achieving your own glory in life. You are God's workmanship, from start to finish. God leads and guides you into the good works that you are to do for him—works that are totally in keeping with the talents, skills, experiences, and abilities he has given you.

When I look back on my life, I stand in amazement at how God has moved me from place to place, from experience to experience, always positioning me to take the next step in my life, always putting me into places and situations so that he might refine or develop something within me that will be useful to his purposes later.

As a teenager I sold newspapers to make money to buy clothes and other things I needed. One night I was talking to a friend named Julian as we stood on a street corner where I was selling newspapers. I told him that I believed the Lord was calling me to preach. I said, "You know, I've got to go to school, and I don't have any money for that." I didn't know this fellow all that well. We were just talking about our lives in a rather casual way. At that precise moment in our conversation, the pastor of my church walked by. Julian said, "Mr. Hammock, Charles believes the Lord has called him to preach. Do you think you can help him go to school?"

Pastor Hammock said, "Well, I might. Why don't you come by and see me?"

I went to his office one day, and it turned out to be one of the most important afternoons of my life. Pastor Hammock arranged for me to receive a four-year full scholarship to the University of Richmond, about 150 miles away from my hometown.

Was it an accident that I happened to be talking to Julian that night? Or that Pastor Hammock walked by? Or that Julian spoke up as he did? No. God was at work in ways I couldn't see.

God is not only our orchestrator, but our composer.

Christ Jesus is the author *and finisher* of our lives. (See Hebrews 12:2.)

As long we insist on writing our own stories, he cannot write his living will onto our hearts.

As long as we insist on forging our own paths, he cannot lead us into his paths of righteousness.

As long as we insist on governing our own lives, he cannot be our sovereign King and Lord.

As long as we insist on living life according to our own desires, he cannot impart his desires or guide us into his wholeness, fruitfulness, and blessings.

As long as we feel that we are in control of our fate, we cannot experience fully the destiny he has for us.

We are *his* workmanship. When we act otherwise, we are breaching our trust relationship with God and are refusing to submit our lives fully to him.

Chapter Four

THE OBSTACLES
TO BROKENNESS

A number of obstacles keep us from realizing that brokenness is part of God's plan. One of the foremost is the viewpoint that the Christian life is something we *do*. If you ask someone to describe a Christian, he very likely will say something like this: "A Christian goes to church, sings hymns, prays prayers, gives money, reads the Bible, and shares his faith with others." Various people will add or emphasize certain activities or behaviors. Some will say, "He's a Christian because he doesn't smoke, drink, or swear." Others will say, "She's a Christian because she doesn't party or sleep around with guys."

The Christian life is not defined by what we *do*.

Rather, it is defined by what Christ Jesus did on the cross and by what we *are* as the result of accepting him as our Savior. The Christian life is ultimately defined by what we are in the process of becoming under the tutelage and by the empowerment of the Holy Spirit.

Now certainly as you become more and more like Christ, your outer behavior will change. Certain behaviors simply will be incompatible with Christ Jesus living his life through you. An overflow of his life in you will manifest itself as service and as acts of praise and thanksgiving to God. A true believer doesn't have to ask, "Now how should I act in order to show myself to be a Christian?" A true believer simply responds to the love of God within himself or herself and then behaves, speaks, and responds to life as Christ would behave, speak, or respond.

The Obstacle of Self-Sufficiency

One of the greatest mental hurdles you may have when it comes to brokenness is adjusting your opinion of what it means to be a Christian and to live a Christ-honoring life. Being a Christian isn't a matter of doing, it's a matter of *being* in relationship with Christ Jesus. The *doing* work is his. He is responsible for transforming us into the image of himself. He is our author and editor, the one who is adjusting our lives so that we conform fully to God's plan for us.

You can't change your sinful nature. You can't look in the mirror one morning and say, "I'm now going to cleanse myself of all my sin and make my life over completely." It simply isn't possible. Many people *try* to change themselves spiritually, and they inevitably come to the same sad conclusion: "I can't do it by myself." Only Jesus Christ can cleanse and change a human heart. Only the Holy Spirit, sent by Christ to dwell in us, can guide our decision making, soften our hearts, and trigger our conscience so that we will make choices and initiate Christlike responses.

We must never forget—we are the clay. He is the potter!

THE OBSTACLE OF TALENTS AND GIFTS

Another main obstacle to our receiving blessing from brokenness is our talents and gifts. In what seems a contradictory truth, our gifts and talents can keep us from using our talents *fully* or from receiving *more* talents and gifts.

Very often, the most gifted have the most difficult time with God's breaking process. The gifted are often the most determined to succeed in life, and they have the most self-confidence. As far as the world is concerned, they are the ones who have the most going for them.

The trouble with gifts and talents is not in *having* them, but in *relying* on them and trusting in them. When we trust in our natural God-given gifts to get us through life, we miss out on the many ways in which God might infuse those gifts with his presence and multiply our gifts far beyond anything that we could do with them.

Those who are satisfied with what they have rarely look to God to supply them with what they truly need.

They don't see what they're missing.

They don't see how God might be using them.

They don't see the fullness of God's design for them.

They don't even realize they are missing out on blessings.

I have found in my pastoral experiences through the years that those who hold tightly to the reins of their own lives are very often those who have many talents or many possessions. They believe they have a lot to lose, and therefore they do whatever is necessary to secure what they have, even to the point of hoarding it or locking it away far from public use or view.

What the highly gifted don't realize is that you can never lose in surrendering your all to God. You can never lose in giving yourself away. The mystery of God's great ability to use our lives lies in this principle, "Give, and it will be given to you. A good measure, pressed down, shaken together and running over, will be poured into your lap. For with the measure you use, it will be measured to you" (Luke 6:38).

This verse does not refer merely to finances or material goods, but to all of one's life. What we give to God, he gives back to us in greater abundance—we are multiplied, and we find renewal, joy, peace, and fulfillment. We simply cannot outgive God.

Neither can you do more with your life than God can do with your life. He made you, and therefore, he knows exactly how to expand you, use you, and fulfill you. He knows all that you are capable of being and doing, and he knows how to fulfill your potential.

So often we find ourselves saying as we look at various careers, jobs, or opportunities that come our way, "I don't know what to do. I don't know which choice to make. I don't know which path to follow."

God knows. He knows not only what we are capable of doing, but how to bring to the surface talents, abilities, and gifts that we don't presently know we have!

When the highly gifted are broken, they often try to fix the situation in which they find themselves by using their own strengths and abilities. The far wiser course is to turn to God and to admit, "You know something about this I don't know. I submit to you. Do with me and my talents whatever you desire to do."

THE OBSTACLE OF MISPLACED TRUST

In fashioning and shaping our lives, God intends to bring every area of our lives into submission to his will. Toward the accomplishment of this purpose, God removes from us every hindrance that keeps us from being fully surrendered to his will and that prevents us from fully trusting him.

God's purpose for our lives is that we trust him completely. As long as we trust anything within ourselves, we aren't trusting him fully. The thing that we trust instead of God—consciously or unconsciously—becomes an obstacle, a stumbling block, a barrier, a hindrance to our trust of God. To use the biblical illustration of the potter and the clay, this thing we trust becomes a stone, a bubble, a flaw, a dry piece of clay that isn't fully pliable.

What are some of these things we trust?

Self

First and foremost, we trust ourselves. We are born with a proud independence. Many people have put out a big sign on the wall of their souls: "God, Keep Out." Others will say to the Lord, "God, you can have this percentage of my life—perhaps even as much as ninety-five percent—but this one area I reserve for myself." We want to go where we want to go, buy what we want to buy, do what we want to do, have the kind of friends we want to have, live where and how we want to live.

God says to us, however, that if we are to have the fullness of his power, wisdom, and love, we must trust him completely and we must reserve no part of ourselves for ourselves.

Wealth

We also trust in money or in material assets. I once knew a man who was very wealthy. He told me jokingly one day, "If I have less than thirty thousand dollars in my checking account, I feel poor."

He had placed his security in money. He began to place more and more emphasis on his business, and less on his family and church relationships. The more he devoted himself to his business, however, the poorer the decisions he made. Several bad investments wiped him out financially. After years of feeling abandoned, his wife left him. He ended up living in a small, dingy, one-bedroom apartment by himself. He tried everything he knew to reverse his financial fortunes, but God didn't let up until this man finally came to the place where he said, "God, I'm yours. I trust *you*. I've been trusting in money all my life. Now I'm going to trust you."

In the aftermath of his brokenness, God restored him to the ability where he makes enough to have his needs met, but the greater miracle in the man's life is that he doesn't *care* about being fabulously wealthy any longer. His identity is no longer tied up in money.

Image and Appearance

Some people trust in their beauty or the appearance of success. They rely on their image to get them through life.

I once knew a woman who had lived her entire life to be beautiful. Even as an older woman, she was beautiful and always very well groomed. Making a good appearance was always very important to her.

In her seventies, she became ill with a degenerative disease. As the disease ran its course, she came to the place in her life where outer beauty didn't really matter to her anymore. What happened instead was a growing inner beauty that even her close family and friends had never witnessed before. As her outer body wasted away, her inner spirit began to shine in a wonderful way. She became an inspiration to every person who visited her because she shared so fully the grace of God at work in her life.

This woman died in peace, with a great joy in her heart. Shortly before she died, she said, "I feel ready to graduate and move on." What a wonderful statement of faith and a recognition that God's breaking process in her had been for her eternal good.

Accomplishments and Reputation

Some people trust in their own accomplishment —their past performance. They rely on reputation to see them through life.

A number of years ago I met a man who was extremely arrogant and proud. He had a mean streak a mile wide. I heard him speak one time, and God spoke to my spirit, "Pray for him." This was the last thing I would have thought to do—I didn't *like* the man.

Some time later, I ran into this man, and he invited me to have dinner with him. I wasn't all that interested in going, but I agreed. As we talked, I found him to be mellow, gentle in spirit. He wasn't at all the man I had known.

He told me his story. The company he had founded had forced him out. He hit rock bottom. But in the process, he turned to God. He yielded to the breaking process and surrendered his life to God. He was still out of work at the time I met him, but everything about this man's personality had changed. I heard a short time later that he founded another company with two partners, and this time, he was operating it according to God's principles of love and respect for his employees and partners.

Anytime we seek to rest on our laurels, we are in danger of being broken. We are trusting in our own past performance rather than in God's providence for the present and future.

THE OBSTACLE OF WANTING TO MAINTAIN CONTROL

What area of your life are you withholding from God today? In what area do you choose to remain in control? What part of your life would you prefer that God ignore? Into which areas of your life would you rather that he not snoop?

Some people I know talk to God about these areas and even admit that they are refusing to yield control of them to God, but they still don't let go. They rationalize their behavior by saying, "Nobody's perfect," or they tell God that since they've been dealing with this area of their lives for a very long time, they are about to conclude that "You must have made me this way, God." The reality is, they don't *want* to submit this area of their life to God.

I know a man who for years smoked two packs of cigarettes a day. He readily admitted to me that he knew smoking was a bad habit and that his health was being affected. I offered to pray with him to ask God to give him the willpower to quit, but he refused the offer. He said, "Oh, I don't think God has any concern about this. It's up to me to quit if I want to quit." It wasn't until this man had been diagnosed with emphysema that he called to ask me to pray for him.

A woman I know has tried for years to become pregnant. She and her husband have spent thousands of dollars seeking out specialists and traveling to fertility clinics. I asked her and her husband one time if they had asked God what his desire for them might be. She laughed as she said, "I'm afraid to ask God about this. He might say he doesn't want us to have children."

We each have these areas of our lives in which we want to maintain total control. And they are *precisely* the ones into which God moves. In fact, these areas that we hold to be off limits to God are the very ones he focuses upon in order that every aspect of our independence be stripped away from us. His desire and purpose for us is *total dependence upon him*. Nothing short of *complete* dependence will suffice.

I love to go out West and roam around in the wilderness. I like to sleep in a tent when it's cold and to photograph nature or hunt. I enjoy the solitude and beauty of the mountain wilderness areas of our nation. On most of my wilderness trips, I contact an outfitter who assigns me a horse for the trek. Sometimes I've had very gentle horses who, with the slightest movement of the reins, have known exactly what to do. Such a horse obeys instantly. Sometimes merely a spoken word will do.

I've ridden other very independent horses! I could pull on the reins, jerk the reins, kick with my stirrups, speak sharply, and *nothing* happened that I wanted to have happen! These horses supposedly had been broken, but as far as I was concerned they were not broken very well. At times, these independent horses have put me into dangerous positions—lunging forward down a hill, balking through narrow passageways. Believe me, I'd much rather have a gentle, well-broken horse anytime, in any situation.

What happens in the breaking of a horse? Contrary to what many people believe, the horse's spirit isn't broken. A well-broken horse remains strong, eager, quick-witted, and aware, and he loves to gallop when given free rein. Rather, it is the horse's *independence* that is broken. The breaking of a horse results in the horse giving instant obedience to its rider.

When a child of God is broken, God does not destroy his or her spirit. We don't lose our zest for living when we come to Christ. We don't lose the force of our personality. Rather, we lose our independence. Our will is brought into submission to the will of the Father so that we can give instant obedience to the one whom we call Savior and Lord.

Now, we can *insist* on having our own way. God doesn't strip us of our free will either before or after our accepting Jesus as Savior. We can "do our own thing" no matter what God says to us or how he may direct us. But when we act independently, like an unbroken or partially broken horse, we put ourselves into danger. His desire is that we *not* experience the consequences of our own willful wandering into sin and the dangers of evil.

Brokenness is the condition whereby our will is brought into full submission to his will so that when he speaks, we put up no argument, make no rationalization, offer no excuses, and register no blame, but instead, instantly obey the leading of the Holy Spirit as he guides us. The end result is one of blessing—it is for our good both now and forever.

THE OBSTACLE OF SELF

When God leads us into or allows us to experience breaking periods, he is after our self-will, self-reliance, self-dependence, self-sufficiency. He's after everything that smacks of self, and of willful independence, in us.

For some, self is all tied up with social status—power, position, authority.

For some, self is inseparable from intellectual prowess or a vibrant "good personality" that always seems to win friends and influence people.

For others, self is tied into appearance or health—beauty, fitness, or energy.

For still others, self is linked most closely to things—possessions, living in the "right" neighborhood.

Our concept of self reveals how much we trust God and have submitted our lives to him.

Ask yourself, "When do I feel good about myself? When do I feel bad about myself?"

If a bad hair day, a poor performance at work, or the loss of a favorite possession throws you into a major sense of loss . . .

If you feel you *must* have compliments from your spouse or friends, or you must achieve a certain degree of financial independence in order to feel valuable and worthy . . .

If you feel you are "nobody" unless you live in a certain way, have certain perks, or are recognized for certain accomplishments . . . you need to reevaluate your trust relationship with God. God desires that our concept of self be totally and completely embedded in his love and his definition of what is worthy and valuable.

The more we cling to the thing we are trusting other than God, the harder the breaking period may be. At times, it seems as if God must wrench from us or shatter within us those things that we trust more than we trust him. The breaking process can be extremely painful. We can know sorrow, hardship, and suffering as we have never known or even imagined.

Our natural tendency when God begins to target an area for breaking in our lives is to cling to that area even more. Generally speaking, we know what it is that we must yield or submit to God. In talking to countless people through the years about God's breaking process in their lives, I have heard repeatedly, "I knew what I was doing was contrary to what God desired for me, but I did it anyway." That feeling may have been intuitive, unspoken, more subconscious than conscious, but nevertheless, there was a knowing that they had withheld an area of their lives from God.

Why are we afraid to let go? Because we don't want to lose control. That's pride in its rawest form.

We are afraid that God won't love us enough to meet our needs, fulfill our desires, or give us contentment. We fear that we will go through life lacking something vital, missing out on something good, or not experiencing something that we desire to experience.

Ask yourself squarely, "How much do you think God loves you?"

I asked one woman this question one day when she came to see me in the wake of her husband's death following a lengthy illness. She was angry with God and finally blurted out, "God abandoned me when I needed him the most."

I assured her that God never abandons us. He assures us always of his presence. I knew that the problem was not that God had abandoned her in her time of trial, but rather, that she had turned to everyone and everything other than God in her time of trial. She had abandoned him. Rather than confront her with this fact, however—which I knew she couldn't accept at that time—I asked her, "How much do you think God loves you?"

She said bitterly, "I don't think he loves me at all."

"I don't believe that's possible," I said. "That would make you the only exception in the history of the entire world."

She seemed stunned. I continued, "First John 4:8 tells us that God is love. Love is the foremost of his attributes. And whatever God has as an attribute, he has as an infinite, pure, and perfect attribute. God's nature doesn't change. If he loves one person, he loves all people."

"Then what happened?" she said. "Why did God let my husband get so sick and suffer so much and die? How could God love me and let that happen?"

"I don't know," I said. "I don't know why God acts as he acts, but I do know that God never stopped loving you, or your husband, for one moment. I suspect that you are angry at God right now because you are afraid that he won't be there to help you in the coming days."

She nodded silently as tears filled her eyes. "I want to assure you," I said, "that God *will* be there for you. I don't know all that God has for you in the future, but I do know this, he desires for you to trust him completely. He desires for you to rely upon him every step of the way, every day, all the way to heaven."

If we believe that God doesn't love us—or that he doesn't love us *enough*—then our tendency is not to trust him. Trust issues are inevitably love issues. Ask yourself today:

- Would God rob you of anything that was for your eternal good?
- Would God break you from anything that would cause you to become what he wants you to be?

- Would God take away from you anything that would bless you spiritually?
- Would God deprive you of anything that would build you up, edify you, strengthen you, and build character into your life?
- Would God steal from you anything that would bring you contentment, peace, and joy?
- Would God take away those things that would help you become the maximum of your potential?

NO!

God does not steal from his children. He doesn't kill or destroy those who love him. He doesn't deprive his children as if playing some kind of cruel joke on them. Jesus said in John 10:10: "The thief comes only to steal and kill and destroy; I have come that they may have life, and have it to the full."

At all times, in every situation and circumstance, God is at work in some area of your life, bringing you to the place where you will *want* to become and to achieve what he wants you to become and achieve. He is molding you to have the desires of your heart because he is fashioning your heart to desire what it is that he wants for you. He is working within your spirit so that you may know his will and be eager to do it. And the Lord acts anytime he finds something within us that must be broken—even shattered—in order for us to become who he created us to be.

THE OBSTACLE OF OUR RESPONSE

We decide the outcome of our brokenness.

We can choose to respond to brokenness with anger, bitterness, and hate. We can rail against our circumstances. We can strike out against those whom we believe have caused us pain. Those options are available to us because we have free will.

The way to blessing, however, lies in turning to God to heal us and make us whole. We decide whether we will yield to him and trust him.

Wholeness is God's intended outcome for our brokenness. When we are whole, we can be fruitful. When we are fruitful, we find fulfillment, peace, and joy in our lives.

Jesus said repeatedly to those who came to him for healing, "Be thou made *whole*." Nothing less will do. We are to trust God fully—as one person once said, "wholly and solely." When we do, he makes us whole.

Chapter Five

WHAT DOES IT MEAN TO BE MADE WHOLE?

When many people think of wholeness, they automatically turn to matters of health, sickness, injury, or death. Wholeness, however, is a matter of harmony—body, soul, and spirit. It is living in such a way that all facets and aspects of our lives are interrelated in a health-giving, sound, and resilient way.

When God breaks us, he does so with the purpose of putting us back together again—better than before, and ultimately, so that we might be whole.

Paul prayed a wonderful prayer for the Thessalonians in which he spoke of wholeness: "May God himself, the God of peace, sanctify you through and through. May your whole spirit, soul and body be kept blameless at the coming of our Lord Jesus Christ" (1 Thessalonians 5:23).

We can always trust God's purpose for us to be wholeness and multiplication, not fragmentation or diminishment.

WHOLENESS INVOLVES ALL OF OUR BEING

Let me share several key principles with you about wholeness. First, we must recognize that we have three aspects to our being—spirit, soul, and body.

The body is the way in which we relate to our environment. We have five senses—we smell, see, taste, hear, touch. We live in a physical shell that allows us to interact with the physical world.

We have a soul—a mind, will, emotions, conscience, and consciousness. We cannot see the soul, but we each know that it is part of us. The soul is our means for relating to other people. We have an awareness of ourselves in relationship to others. At the soul level we can laugh with others, love others, and receive love from others, or we can be jealous, angry, and bitter toward others. We choose with our will and mind how we will act in the world—and largely, how we will act toward other people.

We also have a spirit—the inner person. With the spirit we relate to almighty God.

When Adam and Eve were in the Garden of Eden, they had perfect bodies, perfect souls, and perfect spirits. God placed them in dominion over the physical world, and they lived in perfect harmony with each other and with God.

God said to them about one particular tree in the Garden of Eden, "You must not eat from the tree of the knowledge of good and evil, for when you eat of it, you will surely die" (Genesis 2:17).

They ate, and they died. But what died immediately in that act of disobedience? Not their bodies, because they remained alive for hundreds of years. Not their soul, because they still related to each other and to their children. What died was their capacity to relate to God spiritually. Paul wrote: "As for you, you were dead in your transgressions and sins, in which you used to live when you followed the ways of this world and of the ruler of the kingdom of the air, the spirit who is now at work in those who are disobedient" (Ephesians 2:1–2).

Our sinful state is a state of inner death. A person may do very well in the physical realm, and even do quite well in the soul realm, but unless a person is in right relationship with God through Jesus Christ, he is dead in the spirit realm. Only a believer in Jesus Christ has the potential to be a whole person because unless the spirit is made alive in Christ, the spirit facet of a person is out of sync with the rest of his or her being. We cannot be whole if we have only a good body and good relationship with the physical world, and a good soul and good relationships with other people. To be whole we must have a cleansed spirit and a good relationship with God.

The Bible says that when we receive Jesus Christ as our personal Savior, the Holy Spirit comes to dwell in us. This Spirit of God allows our spirits to be united with God's spirit. Our spirits come to life because he is life! When the Holy Spirit dwells in us, we are given a sensitivity to God, an awareness of him, and a living relationship with him. That relationship allows us to talk to him and him to talk to us. We are open in new ways to understanding the Word of

God and to receiving guidance and direction from the Holy Spirit. We also are more sensitive to sin and to the convicting power of the Holy Spirit. Our spirit has been born anew—we have a new spiritual life!

Here's the problem. The unbelieving world knows nothing about the divine spiritual life. They *think* they are spiritual when they follow a form of spiritual ritual or get into the metaphysical realm, but that is not godly spirituality. Any spirituality apart from the Holy Spirit is spirituality rooted in evil. Mostly, however, the unbelieving world doesn't care about spiritual things. The world's philosophy is, "If it looks good, get it. If it feels good, touch it. If it smells good, have some of it. If it tastes good, eat a lot of it. If it sounds good, keep listening." The world lives by its senses and appetites.

We all have appetites. We have an appetite for beauty—we like to look at beauty and experience it. We all have appetites for food, for water, for sex. We also have appetites related to the soul—we have a need for love, a desire to grow, a longing to learn. We have an appetite for independence and freedom to move and to express ourselves. But as long as a person is without a relationship to God, these appetites run according to their own power. They degenerate into what the Bible calls the "lusts" of the flesh—a voracious greed for all that appears good in the physical and soul realms. Appetites run amok cause many of the problems we see today in relationships, in businesses, in society at large.

The believer in whom the Holy Spirit dwells is one who has a new "control system" in place. The Holy

Spirit puts all of the appetites, desires, and impulses of the flesh and soul under the command of the spirit. The divine order for our own creation—spirit over soul over body— is reestablished. When that happens we can experience wholeness.

The rebellion, therefore, that keeps us from being whole is a rebellion of the spirit. The things that stand as obstacles to our being made whole are ultimately things in the spirit, among them

- lack of trust
- pride
- greed
- anger
- hatred
- bitterness
- fear

For the Lord to bring us to wholeness, he must deal with the areas of our lives that keep us from wholeness. They are at the heart of what separates us from the fullness of God's desire for us.

WHOLENESS IS MORE THAN SKIN DEEP

The trouble many people have is that they don't see the spiritual principles involved in the various situations and circumstances they encounter on a daily basis. Even though they have been born again in their spirits, they continue to live—by force of habit and also by force of will—according to old patterns. They see things only on the surface, and they respond to life superficially.

When we begin to see life the way God sees it, we see that life has an ever-flowing spiritual undercurrent. All of life flows from the spiritual dimension. Our desires and ideas and emotions are motivated by the spirit and flow through the soul for expression through the body. Every act of relating to others—what we say, what we do, who we see, and why—has a spiritual dimension and purpose. In fact, everything we do in the physical, mental, or emotional realm has a spiritual component to it.

When we regard our own brokenness, our natural tendency is to look only on the surface. Our society uses different forms of the word *break* to describe brokenness at the circumstantial or relationship level.

- We say that a person's health is "broken" if they are exhausted or have a serious breakdown.
- When a couple severs their relationship, we say that they "broke up."
- When we suffer financial loss, we say that we are "going broke."

Very often, when we are broken, we limit our perspective on brokenness to the physical or emotional realm.

The more important questions to ask in times of brokenness are these:

- What is happening in the spiritual area of my life?
- What might God be desiring to do in my relationship with him?

- How might God work in this time of brokenness to restore me, renew me, remake me, and remold my relationship with him?
- How might God work in and through this situation or circumstance to bring me to greater wholeness?

These questions bring us squarely back to the purpose of God: a total trust relationship with him so he might use us as whole men and women, strong in spirit and completely obedient to him and subject to his leading.

God's purpose is always accomplished *ultimately* at the spiritual level. Outer circumstances may or may not vary. They certainly change only according to God's timing. Our role in times of brokenness is to submit not only to what God desires to do in our lives, but also to his timetable. Wholeness may not come quickly or easily, but it is worth the wait!

Wholeness Takes Time

Paul wrote to the Corinthians, "Therefore we do not lose heart. Though outwardly we are wasting away, yet inwardly we are being renewed day by day. For our light and momentary troubles are achieving for us an eternal glory that far outweighs them all. So we fix our eyes not on what is seen, but on what is unseen. For what is seen is temporary, but what is unseen is eternal" (2 Corinthians 4:16–18).

When we find ourselves broken, we must be very careful not to attempt to predetermine either the methodology or the timetable for our own recovery. God will reveal his plan and purpose to us step by step. Very rarely does he give insight into the total plan he has for us. We are called to trust him day by day by day.

It may very well seem to us that we are wasting away daily, but if we will look beneath the surface to the inner work God is doing, we are actually growing and being strengthened day by day.

I've seen this happen countless times, very often as people struggle with terminal diseases. Their outer bodies literally seem to waste away. And yet, if they are willing to turn to God and to submit completely to him and trust him with their lives, an inner beauty and spiritual strength begins to develop that far outshadows and far outweighs anything happening in the physical realm. Sometimes their bodies are healed physically, sometimes not. But the far more important thing for eternity is that they be healed in their spirit. When God is at work in our spirits, we must recognize openly that the most valuable facet of our being—truly the eternal facet of our lives—is being strengthened, nourished, and refined. That is the dimension of wholeness that truly counts.

We also must recognize that no matter how long we struggle, our time of trial is only momentary. Even if we have an affliction or time of brokenness that lasts for years, even decades, what is that compared to all of eternity? No mathematical calculation is possible between finite time and infinity. We are wise to keep perspective— what we are experiencing in outer circumstances and situations *will* one day change. What is happening on the inside of us, in the realm of our spirit, is what has the potential to last and remain unchanged.

Paul tells the Corinthians to fix their eyes on what is unseen. That's good advice for us, too, at any time we are broken. No matter how bad things may look, if we submit our lives to God, he is at work creating something good and something lasting. He is making us *whole*, beginning in the unseen spiritual dimension of our lives. He is putting things back into their proper order: the spirit first, the soul second, the physical third.

A number of years ago, I pushed myself to the point of serious physical exhaustion. My physician prescribed rest—not just for a week or two, but for as many *months* as necessary. My associates agreed, and I went to a small island where I had nothing to do but walk the beach and think and pray. That was too much rest! I found it much more therapeutic to return home and to become a "carpenter's helper" to the men who were building my home. Gradually I began to return to my activities as a pastor on a part-time and then full-time basis.

During those weeks and months, I not only found my physical strength returning, but I also gained a new perspective on my life and my work. I faced some tough questions. Was I going to relinquish authority to my key staff members and allow God to work in them and through them, or was I going to burden myself with every decision and the details of every program? Was I going to take time off to rest, or keep a seven-day-a-week schedule? Was I going to learn how to relax and play, or was I going to be an all-work, no-play person?

The real issue was one of trust. Was I going to trust God or myself?

Some six months after I first went away to rest, I entered the pulpit one Sunday morning and said to myself, "I'm back." My energy was back, my perspective was right, and most important, my relationship with God was deeper and richer.

The lasting aspect of that experience was not physical. I still get tired and need rest. The lasting impact wasn't solely in my relationships. I still tend to take on too much and work too hard. The real lasting impact of that experience on me was that I came to a spiritual realization that God is not the copilot of my life; he's the pilot! I yielded total control to him.

The real benefit of those months was that I learned to rest in God. I learned how to relax in his will and let him unfold before me his plan and purposes. I put myself into a position where I now allow God to nudge me in my spirit so that I recognize when I need a break or need to let go. My life is not mine; it's his.

WHOLENESS GLORIFIES GOD

In eternity, you and I will be God's trophies. We are the trophies of his grace; the trophies of Christ's death, burial, and resurrection; the trophies of the Holy Spirit's work in our lives. Our purpose is to bring *him* glory. Our greatest glory lies not in what we can achieve and do on our own, but solely in what we allow the Lord to do in our lives so that we bring him glory. We can never know greater satisfaction or have any greater acclaim than to lay our crowns at his feet and to be presented to him as a work in which there is no shame, fault, flaw, or darkness.

We often lose sight of the fact that this life is preparation for the life to come. In this life we are going to school. The process is one of learning and growing and developing. It is a process of becoming. And when we yield to God's purposes, the process is one of becoming whole. When my will is eventually saddle-busted completely, then I belong heart, soul, mind, body, spirit, and everything to him. When that happens, my life is totally and completely *his* responsibility. I am his to do with as he pleases. And that, my friend, is when the excitement in life truly begins!

Chapter Six

THE DEVELOPMENT OF SPIRITUAL MATURITY

$\mathcal{T}$he path from where we are to where God wants us to be—which is a position of total surrender to him and total wholeness—is one that we call spiritual growth. Its end result or goal is spiritual maturity. God breaks us to mature us.

Spiritual growth has three aspects: change, growth, and brokenness.

CHANGE

First, change is part of the process of maturity. If we are not willing to change, not willing to grow, then we will not grow spiritually. We can't hold onto old ways, old ideas, old feelings, or old erroneous concepts about God, the Holy Spirit, or the Christian life, and still grow into the people that God desires us to be. Maturity requires change and a willingness to embrace positive and beneficial changes.

GROWTH

A second aspect to the maturing process, closely related to change, is growth. Not all change results in growth, but certainly all growth is marked by change. Spiritual maturity means a "growing up" until we are fully Christlike in all of our decisions, thoughts, feelings, and actions. As we read in 2 Peter 3:18, "Grow in the grace and knowledge of our Lord and Savior Jesus Christ."

Everything that grows in the natural world, grows in what scientists call a "growth medium." In scientific laboratories, that growth medium is sometimes soil, sometimes water, sometimes certain chemicals. The growth medium for spiritual maturity is love. We grow spiritually as we love one another. The apostle Paul said,

> Speaking the truth in love, we will in all things grow up into him who is the Head, that is, Christ. From him the whole body, joined and held together by every supporting ligament, grows and builds itself up in love, as each part does its work. (Ephesians 4:15–16)

Our growth is not a growth that moves toward independence. That's a pattern in the natural physical world—children grow up to live independently of their parents. Spiritual growth is marked by increasing dependence upon the Lord Jesus Christ. Ultimate spiritual maturity is a state of total dependence upon the Holy Spirit to govern, guide, and guard our lives.

BROKENNESS

A third aspect of spiritual growth is brokenness. If we are to change and to grow, we must be willing to move away from what has been holding us back, pushing us down, or keeping us from being in a position to receive God's best. We must be willing to give up our hold on the things to which we have been clinging with all our might.

THE BREAKING OF MOSES

Each of these three aspects of maturity is evident in the life of Moses. The story of Moses in the Bible actually begins with the story of Joseph, the son of Jacob, who was sold into slavery by his brothers. Through a sequence of dramatic and difficult circumstances, God intervened, and Joseph rose from being a slave to being prime minister of Egypt.

In his position of national leadership, Joseph was able to spare the nation from the ravages of seven years of famine. This famine was so widespread it extended as far as Canaan, where Joseph's family lived. Joseph's brothers sought food in Egypt, and their quest led to a family reunion. Joseph's family, some seventy people at that time, came down to Egypt and were saved from the famine.

By the time Moses was born, this group of Hebrews had grown into a population of two-and-a-half to three million people. After Joseph died, a king came to power in Egypt who didn't have regard for the Hebrews. He said, "The Israelites have become much too numerous for us. Come, we must deal shrewdly with them or they will become even more numerous and, if war breaks out, will join our enemies, fight against us and leave the country" (Exodus 1:9–10). He put slave masters over the Hebrews to oppress them with forced labor. Even so, the Bible says, "The more they were oppressed, the more they multiplied and spread; so the Egyptians came to dread the Israelites and worked them ruthlessly" (Exodus 1:12–13). To quell the growth of the Hebrews, Pharaoh finally ordered that the boy babies born to the Israelites be killed.

Moses was born after this edict had been given. His mother, however, would not destroy her son. She built a little ark, placed Moses in it, and sent him floating in the Nile River, with his older sister Miriam watching secretly nearby. Pharaoh's daughter, by the providential hand of God, found little Moses in the floating basket and decided to adopt him as her own. When Miriam suggested that she knew a woman who might be a nurse to Moses, Pharaoh's daughter agreed to her idea, and thus, Moses' own mother had the privilege of caring for him in his early years.

Once Moses was grown, he went out one day to where the Hebrews were being forced into hard labor. He saw an Egyptian beating a Hebrew, and he killed the Egyptian and buried him in the sand. He thought no one saw him. To his dismay, when he tried to stop two Hebrews from fighting the next day, one of them said, "Who made you ruler and judge over us? Are you thinking of killing me as you killed the Egyptian?" (Exodus 2:14). Moses realized that his crime had been witnessed and he immediately fled to Midian. For forty long years, Moses worked for his father-in-law Jethro as a shepherd in the desert.

Moses went from Pharaoh's palace, where he lived as a son of Pharaoh, to being an exile and a lowly shepherd in the desert. Surely, Moses was being broken!

What in the life of Moses needed to be broken? Here was a man who was very skilled, who had a tremendous background and credentials, who had prestige and power, promise and position, and virtually inexhaustible resources available to him. He had been given a position by Pharaoh. Surely if we were to choose a person qualified and capable of leading God's children out of the bondage of Egypt and back to the land of Canaan, Moses would have to be one of the leading candidates. He had everything it took, from a human standpoint, to be the leader of his people. Why forty years in the desert?

Because Moses needed to be *changed*. God needed to take Moses from a position of self-reliance to a position of total reliance upon him.

The Hebrews as a whole had been Egyptianized, just as Moses had been. They had adopted much of the Egyptian culture and had even begun to worship the gods of Egypt. After all, they had lived in Egypt for four hundred years by the time Moses came on the scene.

God had to deal with the Egyptianization of Moses so that when God delivered his people from Egypt, God alone would be glorified, and God alone would receive the credit. Then, and only then, could the Hebrews begin to see that they must put their trust solely in God. God's purpose in breaking Moses was with a much larger intent of breaking the Israelites so that he might refashion them once again to be his people.

In breaking Moses, God stripped him of everything he had known as a child and young man. In the process of being driven into the desert, Moses lost his family, his palatial home, his privileges, his prominence, his prestige, his power, his pride. He lost everything.

Moses had known what it meant to be dressed in the finest of clothing, ride in the finest of chariots, be served by the finest of servants, and receive the homage of others. Within a matter of days he found himself on the backside of nowhere tending sheep in humble shepherd's apparel, walking on foot, with no servants and nothing but sheep for company. His home was a tent, not a palace. He worked at common physical labor. In many ways, he was brought into full identification with the rest of the Hebrew people.

Over the years, God also changed much about the spirit and soul of Moses. Moses moved from being self-centered to being God-centered. Moses learned about God's ways and about God's definition of success. He learned that it's better to be somebody in God's eyes and nobody in the eyes of the world, than to be somebody in the eyes of the masses and nobody in the eyes of God.

A STRIPPING AWAY OF EVERYTHING NOT OF GOD

You may be thinking, *Does God do that to everybody he plans to use?* On the one hand, you're not Pharaoh's son, so I wouldn't worry about the details of Moses' life being applied to yours. On the other hand, God does use this same principle in breaking each one of us for his use and purposes. God's purpose in our lives is not to make us famous, prominent, prestigious, or wealthy. His purpose in

our lives is to bring us to the position of absolute nothing-
ness so that we will recognize that all we have of value in
this life is God and God alone.

Now, God may ultimately put you in a position of
wealth. He may give you prominence. But, if that happens,
it will be God's doing and for God's purposes. And if you
are totally dependent on God, if God gives you wealth and
prominence, you won't even care that you're wealthy and
prominent! It will be of virtually no account to you. It will
have no real meaning to you. You will be able to use the
wealth and prominence God has given you solely for God's
purposes, and not for your own aggrandizement.

The Bible doesn't tell us why it took forty years for
God to accomplish the breaking in Moses' life. What we
can count on is that God will break and keep on breaking
us until all resentment, hostility, anger, and self-importance
have been broken out of our lives. God isn't concerned
about how long the process takes, but whether the process
is effective. It may have taken forty years for God to weed
out of Moses' life all the traits that kept him from being
totally and completely useful to God.

It may also have required forty years for certain situations in Egypt to come to a head, or for the Hebrew
people themselves to be so sick and tired of slavery that
they were willing to follow the leader God was going to
give them. There is a *fullness* to God's timing. Again and
again in the Scriptures, we read that "when the fullness of
time had come," God moved to act in certain ways or God
raised up certain people to implement his will. God's
timetable is not our timetable. He uses time like a tool to

accomplish eternal purposes. In the context of eternity, forty years is *nothing!*

Virtually nothing about the breaking of Moses would any of us like to experience. This was an extremely difficult, painful, and life-stripping time for Moses. For four decades, Moses was in the process of being shredded, crushed back down into the potter's wheel, pruned, and chiseled until Moses probably didn't recognize himself. The man he used to be and the man he was at the end of forty years in the desert no doubt seemed like two different people to him.

And that was the point. The Moses whom God sent back to Pharaoh to lead the Hebrews out of Egypt was *not* the man who fled from Pharaoh.

BROKENNESS IS COUNTERCULTURAL

So much of brokenness goes against what we are taught in our culture. We are taught to be self-confident, to make our plans and set our goals, to refuse to move or budge from our purposes. Everything in our culture speaks to us in the same way that Moses' upbringing in Pharaoh's court spoke to him. God's "school" of growth for Moses was much different. In the desert, Moses had to learn to be God-reliant, to let God set the agenda for his life, and to do whatever God asked him to do.

Jesus, of course, is the epitome of reliance upon God. He said to his disciples, "Anyone who has seen me has seen the Father. . . . The words that I say to you are not just my own. Rather, it is the Father, living in me, who is doing his work. Believe me when I say that I am in the Father and the Father is in me" (John 14:9–11).

Jesus was living out God's divine plan. And that is what God desired for Moses. It's also what God desires for you and me.

Someone once said, "A soul is converted in a moment of time, but to become a saint takes a lifetime." Conversion happens instantly. Maturity takes many years.

So often I see Christians struggling to get to what they perceive to be the top—not only of their professions or of the social ladder, but of what they perceive to be the Christian life. They gather and gain and accumulate and assimilate and arrange and amass—all the while building their spiritual resumes and their long list of accomplishments—board memberships, committee assignments, and honors—perhaps with the hope that they will one day be able to hand their resume to God and say, "See what I've done for you."

God's work through brokenness calls us not to accumulate, but to discard. He calls us to get rid of this, get rid of that, rid ourselves of this trait and that habit, give up that desire and that goal, and finally strip ourselves of all self until we say, "All that I am and all that I have is God's. He is in me and I am in him, and that's all that matters."

THE PROCESS OF SPIRITUAL MATURITY IN YOUR LIFE

God may not deal with you in the same way that he dealt with Moses, but he will deal with you in similar ways.

What is it that God is stripping away from your life?

What is it that comes to your mind when you think of being broken?

What is it that you have put between you and total surrender to God? What is it that you trust more than you trust God? What is it that you love more than you love God?

Every person I know has an intuitive understanding of what it is that God is desiring to remove from their lives. They may not be able to express it in that terminology, but they usually can identify what it is that they are afraid to do without, or what it is that they most fear they will lose.

We are to love one another. We are to value one another. But never more than we love God or value our relationship with him.

We are to work diligently and to do good work. But we are never to value our work—not even the work that we would define as "work for God"—more than we value our relationship with God.

We are to serve others and share Christ with others. But we are never to value our ministry more than we value our relationship with God.

God will break us . . . change us . . . and cause us to grow until we reach spiritual maturity, no matter how long it takes or how difficult the process may be for us.

PREPARATION FOR SUPERNATURAL MINISTRY

God uses brokenness to prepare a person for supernatural ministry. This function is reserved for the spiritually mature.

Don't let the word *ministry* confuse you. Every Christian is called to ministry, which is simply service to others. This does not necessarily mean full-time work in a church or religious organization.

A woman once said to me, "All of my friends seem to be called into ministry. I'm just a wife and mother." She said this with a laugh, as if dismissing or diminishing her role as a homemaker.

I said, "You have one of the most noble ministries of all!"

She looked at me with surprise. I said, "Can you name for me any greater responsibility in all of life than raising children to love and serve God? Can you name a ministry that requires more of God's wisdom, faith, patience, and love?"

"I never thought of it like that," she admitted. And then she brightened. "I guess I *do* have a ministry," she said.

Indeed. Just think of all the attributes necessary for children to grow up with a heart for God. Think of the sacrifice, the time, the skill, the knowledge, and the understanding that a mother must have to raise godly children. We must never belittle the responsibility or the role of ministry that mothers have. Suppose Moses' mother had said, "I don't have a ministry." Her ministry was one of the greatest in all history—to provide for the survival of her son and to raise him up to care for his own Hebrew people. She ingrained in him the basic faith in God that never left him and that God himself fanned into a roaring blaze many years later.

Each one of us has a ministry. God has a specific avenue of service designed specifically for the full use of our individual talents, gifts, and skills. He has placed us in a unique time, place, and among specific people to accomplish his ministry. We grow spiritually so that we might minister to others with depth, spontaneity, and gracious generosity.

God caused Moses to mature spiritually so that he could liberate his people from bondage and lead them to a land where they could live in the fullness of God's promises to them. He gave Moses a supernatural ministry. And we too are called to supernatural ministry.

You may have noted that I used the word *supernatural* to describe ministry. That's because if ministry is real, it must be supernatural—God-inspired and God-empowered. Ministry means "service." Anybody can minister to another person's needs. But for a person to be engaged in supernatural ministry means that he or she ministers to others under the direct intervention and involvement of God. Supernatural ministry requires the power of the Holy Spirit.

Now, supernatural ministry doesn't necessarily mean working great miracles or healings. Caring for your business from a foundation of spiritual principles, raising a godly family, preaching the gospel, singing in the church choir, playing in the city orchestra, teaching school, working in a hospital—any number of activities we can name can be done as a supernatural ministry *as long as what we do is done to the glory of God and as long as we invite the Holy Spirit to work through us in serving others.*

Several aspects of supernatural ministry are important to note.

SUPERNATURAL MINISTRY HAS AN OBJECTIVE

God always has an objective in mind when he calls us to a specific supernatural ministry. God spoke to Moses in the burning bush: "I want you to go to Pharaoh and tell him to let my people go." This was the objective of Moses' ministry.

SUPERNATURAL MINISTRY REQUIRES ACTIVE TRUST

The mission that God called Moses to undertake was staggering. Moses immediately sought a way out. He said, in essence, "You've got the wrong fellow." He told God he couldn't speak in public, couldn't accomplish the goal, and asked God to find somebody else. Finally, however, Moses surrendered not only to God, but to the supernatural ministry God had laid before him.

In all of Scripture you won't find a more concise statement of humility: "I can't do it, God." This is where God desires us to be—we can't do it, but as we trust in him, God can.

> *Bear not a single care thyself.*
> *One is too much for thee.*
> *The work is mine and mine alone.*
> *Thy work to rest in me.*
>
> —HUDSON TAYLOR

God calls us to this attitude, to this "faith position."

God never released Moses from actively trusting him. He didn't say, "Well, Moses, you trusted me once, so now I know you will always trust me." To the contrary. Moses' faith was challenged again and again. The more intense the plagues became, the greater the trust Moses needed to have in God. The more difficult the challenges as the Israelites left Egypt, the greater the trust required of

Moses. The longer the years wore on in the wilderness, the greater the need for trust.

We never get to the position in supernatural ministry where our faith is no longer challenged. We are called again and again and again to a position of total surrender, total trust, total yielding, total commitment.

SUPERNATURAL MINISTRY IS EMPOWERED BY GOD

Can you imagine how Moses must have felt when he heard God's ministry objective for his life? *Me? A shepherd? Go into Pharaoh's court—the seat of power that has sought my life for murdering an Egyptian—and tell them to let all of their slaves go? Organize a group of nearly three million people to leave the only home they've ever known to go to a land they've never visited?* God's objective for Moses' ministry was vast and complicated.

No matter what supernatural ministry God calls you to undertake, it will likely seem monumental to you. That's part of God's plan. He wants us to rely on him *totally* for the accomplishment of his objective. If we could do the ministry in our own strength and according to our own wisdom, we wouldn't need God and the ministry wouldn't be supernatural.

God clearly told Moses, "*I'm* going to free them." Moses was to do the telling to Pharaoh, but God was going to do the freeing.

God sent Moses to Pharaoh with only one thing— a shepherd's staff. That staff was a symbol of the presence of God. Moses had been completely stripped of any other "qualifications." He had been reduced to a position of total trust upon God. If God didn't work as God promised he would work, then nothing would happen. The rod in Moses' hand was supernatural because God made it supernatural; the wonders that unfolded when Moses stretched forth the rod had nothing to do with Moses, other than that Moses was obedient in doing what God told him to do with the rod.

Moses didn't convince Pharaoh. He didn't open the Red Sea. He didn't provide food. He didn't provide water. He didn't map out the route through the wilderness. God did. God assumed full responsibility for all the consequences of his actions and all the needs of his people. Moses only had to obey what God told him to do.

Ministry inevitably follows that pattern.

We may plant the seed. But God grows it.

We may provide bandages and medicines. But God does the healing.

We may pray earnestly. But God does the miracle.

We do our part, but then God does the part that only God can do!

The logistics of leading such a large group of people from Egypt to Canaan were staggering. Moses needed to motivate them to go. And then, what about food, water, and supply lines needed for the long march across the desert? What about transporting their baggage? What about crowd control? What about the sick? The stragglers? The reluctant? The rebels? No doubt the life of a shepherd in the desert looked more appealing to Moses the more he thought about what it was that God had called him to do. But God said, "I will be with you. I will cause the elders of Israel to listen to you. I will stretch out my hand and strike the Egyptians with all the wonders that I will perform among them. After that, Pharaoh will let you go. I will make the Egyptians favorably disposed toward this people, so that when you go, you will not go empty-handed." (See Exodus 3:12–22.)

God says the same thing to us anytime he calls us to supernatural ministry. He says, "I'm the one who will do it. I will accomplish the task. You do what I tell you to do, and I will cause it to come to pass." The provision and the power for accomplishing what God calls us to do resides with God. He imparts his power through us to accomplish his objective.

SUPERNATURAL MINISTRY AFFECTS OTHERS

Only God could mature Moses spiritually. The same held true for the lives of the Israelites as a whole. Only God could de-Egyptianize his people. Toward that end, he gave the law, taught them the law, led them through the wilderness, protected them against their enemies, and fed them with manna. He invaded every area of their lives—breaking them and rebreaking them as a people so they might become a *peculiar* people, a different people, a specially chosen people for himself.

In breaking the Hebrews, God separated them from all the pagan, heathen, adulterous people around them—just as he had separated Moses. He called them to a different set of customs, a different mode of dress, a different ritual of worship, a different pattern of behavior. He further commanded the Israelites not to intermarry or have fellowship with those who didn't serve the one true and living God. God gave them their own economy, their own lifestyle, their own set of commandments and laws.

It is no accident that Moses lived in the desert for forty years and then that the children of Israel wandered in the wilderness for forty years. Just as God had de-Egyptianized Moses and turned Moses into his chosen leader of the Hebrew people, so God was de-Egyptianizing his people and turning them into his chosen people.

God gave his people a sign of his presence, just as he had given a sign to Moses—in their case, it was a pillar of cloud by day and a pillar of fire by night.

When the children of Israel finally arrived in the land God had promised to them, they saw God's total provision for them in defeating their enemies. The wall of Jericho fell at the sound of trumpet blasts and shouts from the people. God brought about the victory in a way that gave full glory to God.

And yet there's more. Why did God want to bring his people to spiritual maturity? Again, for supernatural ministry. God had told Abraham that through his family, all the nations of the world would come to know God. They were to be a "light to the nations." (See Isaiah 42:6 and 49:6.)

What a tremendous goal God had set for the Hebrews! Again, just as in the life of Moses, he set before his people a phenomenal objective. He says, "If you do what I tell you to do—if you are totally obedient to me— I will bless you . . . *and make you a blessing.*"

God's purpose for breaking you and bringing you to a place of wholeness and spiritual maturity is so that he might use you as his tool in bringing still others to wholeness and spiritual maturity.

He teaches us so that we might teach others.

He imparts his insights to us so that we might share them with others.

He comforts and encourages us so that we might provide comfort and encouragement to others.

He gives us spiritual gifts so that we might use them to help others.

He gives us financial prosperity so that we might benefit others and provide the means for the Gospel to reach them.

SUPERNATURAL MINISTRY REQUIRES TOTAL SACRIFICE

Those who are broken come to a place of total self-sacrifice. This position of sacrifice is critical to our ability to minister. True supernatural ministry is not halfhearted or superficial. It requires great depth of giving, a total commitment, an overflowing abundance of unending love.

Again and again, the Israelites rebelled against Moses, which was actually a rebellion against God. On several occasions, Moses said in near desperation, "What am I to do with this hard-hearted, stiff-necked people?" God, however, never gave up on them, never gave up on Moses, and gave Moses the strength never to give up on his own people.

We can't have supernatural ministry at work in our lives if we aren't willing to be poured out to others. Supernatural ministry calls for a total giving of one's love, time, compassion, gifts, and loyalty. It means being in a position where nothing is held back.

God's desire is for us to serve, not for us to be served. Jesus clearly taught that the servant is the one who is the greatest of all. Service is to be our life.

It's a matter of being a vase or a bucket. You can have a beautiful vase that's worth thousands of dollars and set it in a prominent place in your home so that you and others can walk by and say, "Isn't that pretty?" Or you can have an old five-gallon bucket and use it to carry water to refresh a lot of people who are thirsty. The same is true for us in ministry. Some folks desire solely to be pretty, looked at, and admired for their "worth." Others are willing to be old buckets, full of God and emptied of self, in order to be of service to others.

We must be willing to get dirty.

We must be willing to roll up our sleeves and work.

We must be willing to sacrifice.

We must be willing to go through stormy times.

We must be willing to suffer on behalf of others.

We can't get to spiritual maturity without suffering and pain, and we can't engage in supernatural ministry without being willing to endure even more suffering and pain. The joy set before us, however, is the joy of knowing that God is with us, that God is working in us and through us, and that God is pleased with us. And friend, there's no greater joy than that.

Moses' ministry was not easy. It took great courage for him to go repeatedly into Pharaoh's court and announce yet another round of doom upon the Egyptians. It took great faith for Moses to lead God's people right up to the edge of the Red Sea—knowing that Pharaoh's armies were rapidly approaching from the rear and they had no obvious way to get across the body of water in front of them. It took great patience for Moses to endure the grumbling and complaining of the people.

If Moses had not been fully broken before God, he could not have endured the supernatural ministry put before him.

You and I cannot survive the supernatural ministry that God calls us to do if we do not remain fully surrendered and yielded to him. God does not bring us to supernatural ministry so that we can do that ministry on our own, once again striving to accomplish great things on our own strength. No! He calls us to continue to surrender our lives to him, day by day, experience by experience, year by year. We must *remain* in a position of total surrender and commitment.

I once overheard a man say, "I'm satisfied with just being saved. I just want to make it inside heaven's gates."

How sad! I thought. *What a tragic waste!* God doesn't save us solely so that we can "barely get in" to his presence or into heaven. He saves us so that we might be brought to spiritual maturity and used by God to fulfill his plans and purposes. The good news for us is that supernatural ministry is what gives our lives a sense of fantastic, indescribable, awesome purpose and meaning.

How many people ask themselves again and again throughout their entire lives, "Why am I here? What is my purpose for being alive?" The person whom God has broken and who has been made whole and brought to spiritual maturity knows the answer to that question. We are here so that God might use us to bring glory to himself! We are here so that God might call us into paths of supernatural ministry that will bring about the accomplishment of his plan for all humankind. We are here to be blessed by God so that we might be a blessing to others!

Once we realize the reason for our existence and begin to walk in it, nobody has to prompt us to get up in the morning. We can hardly wait to work toward the goals God has set before us. There's a joy to our steps, a feeling of hope in our hearts, and a desire to put our shoulders to the wheel and trust God with the outcome!

But first, you must be willing to be broken, to change, to grow. Before God can use you mightily, he must know that you are completely surrendered to him.

Chapter Seven

THE PROCESS
OF BREAKING

$\mathcal{B}$eing broken is a very systematic process, from God's point of view. We see only the chaos of brokenness—we feel the pain, confusion, and disorientation. God, however, doesn't react to life's circumstances. He is fully aware of what is happening to us even before it happens, and he works within and through circumstances to accomplish his purposes. God never loses control of the breaking process.

The life of the apostle Peter gives us a clear illustration of the principles God uses in breaking a person. Perhaps the most famous scene in Peter's life happened the night before Jesus was crucified.

Peter followed Jesus after he was seized in the Garden of Gethsemane and taken into the house of the high priest. As Peter sat in the courtyard of the high priest's house, a servant girl looked closely at Peter and said, "This man was with him." Peter denied knowing Jesus.

A little later someone else saw him and said, "You are one of them." Again, Peter denied the association. About an hour later yet another person said, "He was with him."

Peter replied, "I don't know what you're talking about!" At the moment of this third denial, a rooster crowed. Jesus had predicted that Peter would disown him three times before the rooster signaled the dawn of the next day, and it happened just as Jesus said. (See Luke 22:54–62.)

Peter was not a normal fellow. He was very talented and gifted in many ways. The Gospels name Peter many more times than any other apostle. His name is mentioned in numerous places in Acts, as well as in other books in the New Testament. He clearly was a leader among leaders. Along with James and John, he was part of Jesus' inner circle, one of the men in whom Jesus confided and with whom he shared the most intense and dramatic moments of his life.

Peter was a fisherman, rather impulsive, strong-willed, outspoken, and strong physically. The phrase "self-centered" was written all over him.

You may wonder why Jesus would choose a fellow like Peter.

Jesus chose Peter for the same reason God chooses you and me—he sees all we *can* be. He chooses us for our potential to become like Christ. Jesus chose Peter because he believed he had found a man through whom he could work. He had a special purpose for Peter's life, and he poured himself into Peter to prepare him for the supernatural ministry

God had for him. Like all of us, Peter had areas of his life that needed to be broken so that they might be refashioned and remade. Jesus was willing to engage in that process in Peter's life. In fact, he said to Peter, "I'm going to change your name." In changing Peter's name, Jesus broke the identity of the old Simon—his name at the time Jesus called him to be an apostle—and created a new identity. Simon the reed was in the process of becoming Peter the rock.

The following four key aspects in God's breaking process are applicable not only to Peter's life, but to your life and mine.

GOD TARGETS THE AREA

God targets the area in each one of our lives that needs to be broken.

Each of us has strengths and weaknesses. And very often, God targets what *we* see as a strength in our lives. Why? Because we are much less prone to submit our strengths to him. When we become aware of our weaknesses, we turn to God and say, "I'm weak in this area, please be my strength." But for those areas in which we are strong, we say, "Well, I can handle this on my own." We fail to turn to God and seek his help or his control.

For example, a person who is gifted in teaching or public speaking may not even seek God's help if he or she is called upon to teach a particular Sunday-school lesson or speak before a church group. In comparison, a person who has never taught or who has always felt inadequate speaking before a group is more likely to ask for God's help if he or she is given such a task.

Each of us also has attitudes, habits, and relationships. If any of those attitudes, habits, or relationships are contrary to what God desires for us, they are areas subject to being broken. For example, God will always confront idolatry, greed, addictions, and racial prejudice.

Each of us has desires. If we have a strong desire for something, to the point where we cling to it and consider it even more valuable than our relationship with God, this desire is subject to being broken. We may not readily realize these desires. A good question to ask is this: "What do I spend most of my time thinking about?" The focus of our thoughts and daydreams is very likely a desire. If this desire looms larger in our lives than our desire to know God better and to serve him more fully, God will no doubt address it.

At any given time in our lives God identifies the single most devastating and potentially damaging hindrance to our relationship with him. When he strips away from us something in which we have trusted or something we have loved deeply, we are often devastated. It is our unhealthy love for the thing that is stripped from us which made it a target area. It isn't that God doesn't want us to trust other people or to love them—not at all! God doesn't want us to trust or love others *more than we love him*. Repeatedly in the Scriptures we find the phrase "jealous God." God is jealous for our affection, our love, our time, our desire. He wants to be the number-one priority in our lives.

Jealousy is our ardent desire to possess and protect something that is rightfully ours. A husband may be jealous when someone attempts to woo away his wife because his wife is rightfully *his wife*. A wife may be jealous of those women who might try to woo away her husband. We are *jealous* when someone attempts to take something away from us that truly belongs to us.

Envy is different. Envy relates to possessions or relationships that are not rightfully one's own. We are *envious* when we covet or desire something that genuinely belongs to someone else.

We belong to God. He is our creator. We are his workmanship, his creation, his children. He is jealous of anything and anyone that attempts to woo us away from him and to replace him in our lives.

God wants us to rely completely on him. He wants no relationship to be a substitute for our relationship with him. God crushes, breaks, shatters, and removes anything from our lives—very often something dear to us, cherished by us, held tightly by us, counted as valuable to us—that separates us from his love or that forms a barrier between us and God.

We often know what it is that God is likely to target. I strongly suspect that as you have read this book thus far, you have already identified something in your own life about which you can say, "That's something God has probably drawn a circle around as a target for brokenness." We know when something hinders a free flow of the Spirit of God in us. We know when something stops us from witnessing or from having victory in our daily lives. We know when something consumes our attention, disrupts our peace, or magnetizes our thinking. God certainly knows when this happens, and he knows far sooner and more completely than we know it!

Jesus saw severe hindrances in Peter's life.

In Matthew 14, Jesus came to his disciples, walking on water, and at the sight of him, the disciples were filled with fear. Peter said, "Lord, if it's you, tell me to come to you on the water."

Jesus said back to him, "Come."

But when Peter got out of the boat and started walking on the water toward Jesus, he took his eyes off Jesus and put them onto the wind and stormy waters. He became filled with fear, began to sink, and cried, "Lord, save me!" (vv. 22–30).

Jesus knew that Peter's impetuous, volatile nature was subject to intense faith . . . or to intense fear. He needed to break the fear cycle in Peter's life if Peter was to follow him without wavering.

In Matthew 16 Jesus explained to Peter and the other disciples that he must go to Jerusalem, suffer many things at the hands of the elders, chief priests, and teachers of the law, and that he must be killed and on the third day be raised to life. Peter took Jesus aside and rebuked him, saying, "Never, Lord! This shall never happen to you!" Jesus turned and said to Peter, "Get behind me, Satan! You are a stumbling block to me; you do not have in mind the things of God, but the things of men" (vv. 21–23).

Jesus knew that he must break in Peter that desire to have things go Peter's way, rather than God's way.

In Matthew 18, Peter asked Jesus, "Lord, how many times shall I forgive my brother when he sins against me? Up to seven times?" Peter thought he was being very generous. Jesus replied, "I tell you, not seven times, but seventy-seven times" (vv. 21–22).

Jesus knew that he needed to break Peter's smug self-righteousness and replace it with the unending generosity of God's forgiveness.

In John 13, Jesus attempted to wash Peter's feet in the upper room. Peter said, "No, you shall never wash my feet."

Jesus replied, "Unless I wash you, you have no part with me."

Jesus knew that he needed to break Peter's pride.

In Matthew 26, Jesus said to his disciples, "This very night you will all fall away on account of me, for it is written: 'I will strike the shepherd, and the sheep of the flock will be scattered.' But after I have risen, I will go ahead of you into Galilee."

Peter said, "Even if all fall away on account of you, I never will." He vowed to die with Jesus before he would ever disown him (vv. 31–35).

Jesus knew that he needed to break Peter's egotistical assumption that he was above what Jesus had prophesied.

In Luke 22, armed men came to arrest Jesus in the Garden of Gethsemane; Judas betrayed Jesus with a kiss. Peter struck the slave of the high priest, cutting off his right ear. But Jesus responded to the situation by saying, "No more of this!" He touched the man's ear and healed him.

Jesus knew that he needed to teach Peter that the kingdom of God is not to be established by force, but by the power of love alone.

Again and again, Peter was broken. Bit by bit, in situation after situation, Jesus acted to pulverize the pride, egotism, and self-sufficiency of Peter.

He will do no less in our lives. God will target the areas that keep us from trusting him completely and yielding to him fully.

GOD ARRANGES THE CIRCUMSTANCES

Just as the target area for brokenness is subject to God's will, so are the circumstances that lead to our being broken.

Why did Jesus walk on water? In part, he was setting up the situation in which he could teach Peter and the other disciples about using their faith to overcome fear.

Why did Jesus wash the feet of his disciples? In part, he was setting up the situation to confront Peter's pride.

Why did Jesus prophesy that his disciples would deny knowing him? In part, he was setting up the situation for Peter to confront his own arrogance.

These circumstances no doubt ended up being painful for Peter each and every time. Stop to consider the situation: Each time Jesus chiseled away at Peter's pride and self-sufficiency, he did so publicly. Peter was humiliated, embarrassed. Peter was brought to the place where he wept bitterly in recognizing that he had denied Jesus. He suffered. He agonized over his failure and his lack of trust in God.

The more strongly we put our trust in something, the more tightly we grasp something, the more intensely we love something *other than God* . . . the greater the likelihood that the circumstances God will use in breaking us will be ones that shatter us publicly.

God brings about the circumstances of our breaking in two ways. At times, he engineers the situation that will cause us to confront what he desires to change in our lives. At other times, God will simply allow us to follow the pathway of sin that we have chosen. He will give us enough leeway and enough rope so we can entangle ourselves.

This is especially true with sin against others. The person who abuses others will ultimately be exposed. The person who engages in pornography or illicit sexual behavior will eventually suffer from that behavior coming to light. The person who embezzles funds or willfully mismanages money will find himself in prison. In these cases, God doesn't have to arrange any of the details that will bring about our downfall. We cause our own undoing.

I once knew a man who had an affair with his secretary. When the situation came to light, he was devastated. This man was used to being in control of all situations, in control of his emotions, in control of his career. In seeking to maintain absolute control in his life, he often abused people emotionally and manipulated them to do his bidding. Suddenly, he couldn't control the circumstances. His life exploded in his face.

God is working in his life. He is facing not only his sexual sin, but also his attempt to control his own life. He had not surrendered his will to God's will. Therefore the breaking of this man happened publicly, very likely because his prior manipulation and control of people had been very public.

Whether God brings about the breaking circumstances in our lives or simply allows us to continue to engineer our own breaking circumstances, we eventually come to the place where we are forced to say, "Okay, God. I'll do it your way."

GOD CHOOSES THE TOOLS

God targets the area that needs to be broken. He arranges the circumstances that lead to our breaking. And God chooses the tools with which to break us.

We don't like those tools any more than we like the circumstances with which God chooses to break us.

If I could choose the tool I would like God to use in breaking me, I'd say, "God, please just give me a book. Show me the two pages that speak directly to what it is that you want me to change, and I'll get the message." God has never once operated that way in my life.

Instead, God has used the hurtful remarks or false accusations of people, erroneous negative reports, or people who have attempted to manipulate situations for their own benefit. He has used great challenges, which have initially seemed overwhelming or potentially devastating.

We don't choose the tools God uses. He chooses. Just as we can't tell God when to break us, we can't tell him how to break us. The selection of methods is his business—it's totally beyond our control.

For several years, God has been in the process of breaking a man I know. The tool God is using is the media. This man is continually hounded by the media for what he says and does. He thinks the media is "out to get him." In truth, I believe God is out to change him. Pride in his life says, "I'm above the media. They have no right to scrutinize my life. They have no right to expose what it is that

I'm doing." His arrogance and self-determination are contrary to total surrender to God.

I don't know what tools God may be using in your life to bring you to the place where you will say, "God, I'm yours. No matter what happens to me, I am going to trust you and do whatever it is that you lead me to do." I can tell you this with a fair degree of certainty—the tool will be sharp, painful, and unavoidable. You will not be able to escape it. You will be *forced* to confront the area in your life that needs to be changed. There's simply no way to avoid facing the barrier that stands between you and your total reliance upon God.

Is Death a Tool?

Hear me closely on this. I am *not* saying that God will kill someone you love—a spouse or a child—to get your attention. I don't believe we can ever say that God kills one person in order to get another person to submit to him. In some cases, the death of a loved one results in a person drawing closer to God, but I don't believe that God causes the death of one person to bring about submission in another person's life. Why? Because God loves both you and the other person! He does not bring about calamity or death in one person's life to bless another's.

Furthermore, death is the final blow of Satan. He is the one who brings about death. Does God allow death? Yes, it's part of the curse that still remains on the earth from the sin of Adam and Eve. The Scriptures tell us that it is man's destiny to die (Hebrews 9:27). At the same time, however, God is not the author of death. He is the redeemer of it. Jesus is our resurrection, not our assassin.

For the believer in Christ Jesus, however, death is not a curse. It is a transition into God's eternal presence. The death of a loved one causes us pain because we are separated from someone we love. But death is not final for the Christian believer. One day we will see our departed loved ones in Christ, and we will never be separated from them again. Jesus is victor over death and the grave. His resurrection from death paved the way for our resurrection.

While I do not believe that God causes death to break us, I do believe that he sometimes causes the loss of something very important to us, such as a relationship. Loss is virtually always a part of being broken.

Is Sin a Tool?

Just as I do not believe God causes the death of a person to force another person to submit, neither do I believe that God ever causes a person to sin to bring about submission in another person. For example, I would never claim that God caused a son to get on drugs, or a daughter to engage in a premarital sexual affair, to break either that child or the child's parents. God is not the author of sin. He does not tempt us to sin—Satan does. God does not compel us to sin—we have a free will to respond or to resist temptation.

At the same time, God will take advantage of our weaknesses and sins and disobedience—or those of someone close to us—to bring about a positive change in our lives. He never wastes an opportunity to cause us to grow and mature.

Our Brokenness Affects Others

We must remember that we are not broken privately or in solitary confinement. We are not broken in seclusion, as if we were in an isolated capsule. When God breaks us, our brokenness affects others around us. In turn, the breaking process in the lives of others may affect us.

For example, if God is breaking a man who has allowed his love for his job or business to take precedence over his love of God, and he chooses to break that man by causing his business to fail, the man's wife and children will be affected by the business failure. While the wife and children had no part in bringing about brokenness in the man's life, they not only will be affected by his brokenness, but God will *use* the situation to bring about a refinement in their lives. Nothing is ever wasted in the breaking process. Every person who is affected by one person's brokenness will have an opportunity to face the state of their own spiritual maturity and their own lack of wholeness or lack of trust in God.

I hope you will recall what I said in the very first chapter. God does not bring about brokenness in our lives because he is ruthless, cruel, or hard-hearted. He does not break us out of some perverse desire to injure, maim, or destroy. God is breaking us to get our attention and to deal with some aspect of our lives that keeps us from experiencing the fullness of what he has planned for us.

Our Enemies as Tools

Perhaps the worst tool that God uses in our lives to break us—worst, from our perspective—is our enemy.

Sometimes God will use our enemies to persecute us, and he allows them to keep the pressure on us until he has our full attention and full compliance.

We pray against the assault from our enemies. We cry out, "God, why is this happening to me? Why don't you stop this person? Why don't you deal with my enemies?" All the while, God is allowing the persecution in order to bring us to a position of complete reliance and trust.

If someone is a constant irritant to you—perhaps someone who continually ridicules you, contradicts you, fights you, or speaks ill of you to others—ask God, "What is it that you are trying to teach me through this? Please show me what it is that you are trying to refine in me."

Very often, God reveals rather quickly what it is that he desires for us to learn, do, or change. He doesn't deal with our enemies as much as he deals with us! Often, as soon as we come to grips with what it is that God is seeking to break within our hearts, our enemy ceases to be a problem.

Now, please note carefully that I didn't say that our enemies are right. They may be acting toward us in a way totally opposite to God's commandments. Neither did I say that our irritation against our enemies is unwarranted or unnatural. What I am saying is that God uses our enemies as tools to bring about something *good* in our lives. Once his purpose in us is accomplished, he deals with our enemies on our behalf. We can trust him to exact whatever vengeance is necessary (Romans 12:19).

Our Family as Tools

The family is one of the foremost crucibles that God uses to grind away those traits in us that are unlike Christ Jesus. We don't like it when God uses our spouse to bring about further refinement in our lives. We don't like it when our children point out our flaws, or rebel against us in ways that force us to come to grips with our own rebellion against God.

GOD CONTROLS THE PRESSURE

Just as God chooses the target, sets up the circumstances, and selects the tools for our brokenness, so he controls the amount of pressure we are under. He knows exactly how much pressure is enough to break us—an amount that varies from person to person.

God sets limits on our brokenness. These limits cover both how long the brokenness continues and the amount of pain and suffering we experience. God limits the amount of hurting he will allow you to do.

God causes brokenness to come to an end when one of two points is reached:

One, brokenness ends when our will is broken and we yield to God in submission. The moment you surrender completely to what it is that God desires to accomplish in your life through brokenness, the circumstances related to your brokenness begin to be reversed and the tools of God's breaking begin to be removed.

Two, brokenness ends when it reaches an intensity when it will damage God's purpose for your life. God will not allow you to be broken or shattered to the point where you cannot engage in the supernatural ministry he has prepared for you. That would be utterly counterproductive. His purpose is to train you, mold you, refashion you—not to destroy you.

Resistance Prolongs the Process

Our resistance to God's breaking process prolongs it. Our willingness to yield early shortens it. This is the only area in the breaking process that we can impact. We don't choose the targets, dictate the circumstances, or choose the tools—but we can determine how intense the pressure will build and how long the process will continue by our willingness to yield to God. The earlier we identify what it is that God is doing in our lives and yield to it, the better it is for us.

When we resist the breaking process, God must turn the vise a little tighter, chisel a little deeper, sand a little stronger.

Those who resist God long enough are not destroyed—rather, they generally are "shelved." They are ignored. They remain unused. They stagnate at their current level of growth and spiritual maturity. They remain in their flawed state.

A woman once said to me, "It's been years since I felt God was truly using me. I used to be very active in the church, but in recent years, it seems that I'm increasingly uninvolved. Does the Lord still have something for me?"

I asked her, "When was the last time you truly felt the Lord was trying to change something in your life?"

She said, "Oh, I'm not sure he's ever tried to change something in me."

I said, "Have you ever had any great problems in your life—difficulties that seemed to pull the rug out from under your feet emotionally, spiritually, perhaps even physically?"

"Oh, yes," she said, "but I just waited them out."

"Did those problems change anything in you?" I asked.

"No," she said with great resolution. "I'm a survivor. I didn't change a bit. I stuck to my guns."

I said, "That's likely the problem. As long as you refuse to recognize the ways in which the Lord desires for you to grow and change, the Lord can't trust you to do his bidding. He loves you so much that he doesn't want you to stay the way you've always been. He wants you to grow up into the exact likeness of Christ Jesus. He has a great and wonderful purpose and plan for your life, but he can't bring you into the fullness of it as long as you refuse to grow and change in your spirit."

Broken But Not Destroyed

God's purpose is to break our will, not our spirit. His purpose is not to destroy us, but to bring us to a position of maximum wholeness, maturity, and usefulness in his kingdom. He wants us to yield control of our lives to him.

The last thing in the world that Peter wanted to give up was control. He wanted to dictate whether his feet would be washed, the terms by which he would prove Jesus was indeed walking on the water, the way Jesus was going to become the Messiah.

We are like Peter—each one of us has a very difficult time giving up control. We always want to have the final say. Brokenness is God's process of bringing us to the point where we not only don't have the final say, we have nothing to say, except to ask, "Lord Jesus, what would you have me to do?"

It took three years for Peter to come to the place where he was willing to say to Jesus, "Yes, I'll be and do what you want me to be and do. I give up control to you."

After the crucifixion of Jesus, Peter returned to fishing. Jesus found him there by the seashore one morning, and he said to him, "Peter, do you love me?"

Three times Jesus asked the question and three times Peter said, "Lord, you know I do!"

Jesus gave Peter something very specific to do: to feed and care for "the sheep"—the followers of Jesus who were in need of a leader. Peter finally yielded fully to what it was that Jesus desired for him. The Lord had given him a supernatural ministry objective, and on the day of Pentecost, he gave Peter supernatural ministry empowerment.

Listen to what Peter eventually wrote: "God opposes the proud but gives grace to the humble" (1 Peter 5:5). He was quoting Proverbs 3:34 in his letter. Peter *knew* the reality of that verse in his life.

The following poem speaks to the breaking process that Peter experienced and that we all experience:

> *When God wants to drill a man,*
> *And thrill a man,*
> *And skill a man*
> *To play the noblest part;*
> *When He yearns with all His heart*

To create so great and bold a man
That all the world shall be amazed,
Watch His methods, watch His ways!
How He ruthlessly perfects
Whom He royally elects!
How He hammers him and hurts him,
And with mighty blows converts him
Into trial shapes of clay which
Only God understands;
While his tortured heart is crying
And he lifts beseeching hands!
How he bends but never breaks
When his good He undertakes;
How He uses whom He chooses,
And with every purpose fuses him;
By every act induces him
To try his splendor out—
God knows what He's about.

—Unknown

God makes no mistakes in the breaking process. He knows precisely what areas to target in our lives. He knows what circumstances to arrange to break us, and what tools to use. He knows how much pressure we can take. He is about the task of *perfecting us.*

The good news is that God never does anything less than a perfect work in us, if we will only yield to his will.

Chapter Eight

OUR PROTEST AGAINST BROKENNESS

*M*any people today believe they can run away from God, resist his claim on their lives, and live their own way. They believe they can sin and escape the chastisement of God. They are wrong.

A price must be paid for rebelling against God.

Rebellion is not something limited to those who participate in protest marches, engage in terrorism, or run away from home. We each have a rebellious streak, which we manifest in our own unique ways. We each have times when we don't want to give up our way, don't want to yield, don't want to have our wills broken by God. This rebellious streak in us resents and resists God.

Jonah the prophet refused to be broken by God or to yield to God's desire in his life.

When God called Jonah to go to the city of Nineveh and tell the people of their wickedness, Jonah went to Joppa and boarded a ship for Tarshish, a city about two thousand miles in the opposite direction (Jonah 1:1–3).

Jonah didn't want to do what God wanted him to do, and he attempted to run away and hide from God. This tactic didn't work for Jonah. Neither does it work in our lives.

How Can We Run from God?

Stop to consider the futility of trying to run from God. How do you run from the presence of God when everything that is in existence—everybody that is alive, every place, not only on this globe but everywhere in the universe—is always everlastingly in the presence of God? Only someone with a deceived mind thinks he or she can run from God and escape his presence. Running away from God is like running from your own heart. You can't escape and remain alive.

When God begins to tighten his hold on us—to close in on us with specific circumstances, callings, and situations—we often try to escape. We are all like Jonah. We may not be called to Nineveh, but in nearly all cases of brokenness, we initially seek to resist being and doing what God desires for us to be and do. We seek a means of escape.

Let me set the stage for Jonah's story. Nineveh was a great city located about five hundred miles northeast of Jerusalem. The capital of the Assyrian empire, Nineveh was known for beauty, grandeur, greatness, and power. The Ninevites were fierce warriors with a reputation for atrocious torture of their captives. At the time of Jonah, the Assyrians were gobbling up little nations and people who surrounded them; it was only a matter of time before Israel would be attacked. Jonah knew this, and he had a very difficult time with God's call to go to such a place and preach God's punishment to such a treacherous people.

In essence, God was asking Jonah to go to his enemies and preach repentance. Jonah wanted to see the Ninevites punished, not saved (Jonah 4:1–3).

Jonah would rather have died himself than to see his enemies repent of their ways and be spared by God! Jonah was so hostile and angry toward the Assyrians that he was willing to disobey God and to die in his disobedience. He went to Joppa and bought a ticket to Tarshish, generally believed to be a city located in what is now Spain.

Has God ever required of you something about which you said, "Lord, I'm not going to do it," or "Lord, I'll do that later but not now"? Sometimes our rebellion takes the form of saying, "Lord, I know what you're telling me to do, but I think I found a better way to do it." Unless we willingly choose to obey God *explicitly* and *immediately*, we are in rebellion.

YOUR REBELLION BRINGS ABOUT IMMEDIATE RESPONSE

God responds immediately to our acts of rebellion. He sends a storm into our lives, just as he did in the life of Jonah. No sooner was Jonah out to sea on his way to Tarshish than a fierce storm arose and the ship on which Jonah sailed was about to sink. The crew began throwing things overboard in an attempt to lighten the ship and ride out the storm. Jonah was asleep in the hull of the ship. He was doing his best not only to run from God, but to ignore God.

The captain finally went to Jonah and awoke him, saying, "How can you sleep? Get up and call on your god! Maybe he will take notice of us and we will not perish." There is no mention that Jonah even whispered to God. The storm continued to rage.

When we rebel against God, some may come to us and question what we are doing. If that happens in your life, listen to those who attempt to warn you of the danger you are in!

I recently heard about a man who began to date a woman shortly after the death of his wife. She was a woman who had had two children out of wedlock and who had been married and divorced twice. She had a reputation for loose living. The longer he dated her and the more serious he became about her, the more his friends and relatives went to him, saying, "She's not right for you." He ignored all of their warnings.

One day this woman insisted that he give her the deed to his house as a sign of his love for her. When he refused, she began to yell at him and hit him. In the course of defending himself and attempting to control her arms that were flailing in his direction, he caused some bruises on her arms. She called the police, and he was arrested for assault.

That brought him to his senses. He later admitted, "I was in complete rebellion to God. God had told me that I wasn't to become involved with this woman, but I was angry with God over the death of my wife, who had been my childhood sweetheart and with whom I had been happily married for more than thirty years. I ignored the advice of my godly friends. And I paid the price."

Fortunately, he repented of his rebellion before any lasting damage could be done to himself or his children.

Jonah's situation didn't turn out as well. The sailors finally concluded that the storm must be a punishment for someone onboard. They cast lots to see who brought the storm on them. In all likelihood, they put stones into a little bag—one black one and the rest white. Each person pulled out a stone, and the one who got the black stone was considered to be the culprit. Sure enough, the black stone was pulled by Jonah. The sailors asked him, "Who are you?"

Jonah replied, "I am a Hebrew and I worship the Lord, the God of heaven, who made the sea and the land."

The sailors then asked, "What have you done?" Jonah admitted to them that he was running from the Lord.

"What should we do to you to make the sea calm down for us?"

Jonah said, "Pick me up and throw me into the sea, and it will become calm. I know that it is my fault that this great storm has come upon you." (See Jonah 1:8–12.) Even in the face of churning waters and fierce winds, Jonah still remained resolute that he would rather die than preach a message of repentance to his enemies.

The sailors were reluctant to do as Jonah said. They did their best to row back to land, but the sea became even more wild. Finally, they cried out to the Lord, asking him not to hold them accountable for their deed, and then they threw Jonah overboard.

Awaiting Jonah in the stormy waters was a great fish, which, the Bible says, God provided. I don't know what kind of fish that was—it may very well have been a whale since there are whales large enough to swallow small cars. The fact is, God *provided* the great fish to swallow Jonah. He allowed for Jonah to live within that fish. Try as Jonah might, he couldn't seem to die. God had a purpose for Jonah that hadn't yet been accomplished. He was in the process of breaking Jonah, not killing him. God didn't want Jonah dead; he wanted him alive and preaching in Nineveh!

At the end of three days and three nights in that great fish, Jonah prayed to the Lord. He prayed the prayer of a man who was yielding to brokenness. He declared to God that what he had vowed, which was to be God's prophet, he would do (Jonah 2:1–9).

Jonah finally submitted his will completely to God. He yielded fully. And the Scriptures say, "The LORD commanded the fish, and it vomited Jonah onto dry land" (Jonah 2:10).

Jonah went to Nineveh. He walked the city for three days proclaiming, "Forty more days and Nineveh will be overturned."

Jonah didn't cry out God's words in love. He was simply being obedient. He had yielded his will to God, but not his attitude. He spoke in anger, not compassion and mercy. He was willing to do what God told him to do, but in his heart of hearts, he didn't really want to see the people converted. His motive was wrong even though his words were right.

Jonah's will had been broken and was submitted to God. Now God moved in on Jonah's attitude.

The Ninevites, much to Jonah's dismay, received Jonah's message. They believed God, declared a fast—"all of them, from the greatest to the least"—and put on sackcloth in repentance. Even the king of Nineveh rose from his throne, took off his royal robes, covered himself with sackcloth, and sat down in the dust. He decreed that no person should eat or drink, but rather, be covered with sackcloth and call urgently on God. He decreed, "Let them give up their evil ways and their violence. Who knows? God may yet relent and with compassion turn from his fierce anger so that we will not perish" (Jonah 3:8–9).

God was using the Ninevites as a tool in Jonah's life, but he was also using Jonah as a tool in the lives of the Ninevites. Unlike Jonah, however, the Ninevites responded quickly to God's breaking process. They repented immediately. And the Bible says, "When God saw what they did and how they turned from their evil ways, he had compassion and did not bring upon them the destruction he had threatened" (Jonah 3:10).

God's breaking of the Ninevites was accomplished. His work in Jonah was not, however. Jonah still wanted to die rather than live with the knowledge that the Ninevites had repented and been spared. He remained angry at God and angry at the Ninevites. God asked him, "Have you any right to be angry?"

Jonah didn't answer the question. Instead, he sat down at a place east of the city and waited to see what would happen. In attempting to deal with Jonah, the Lord again provided a lesson for him—a vine grew quickly to provide shade for Jonah. But then at dawn the next day, a worm chewed the vine until it withered. When the sun rose, a scorching east wind blew and the sun blazed so hot that Jonah grew faint. Rather than be grateful to God for the vine, or yield to the lesson of the worm and the scorching wind, Jonah still said, "It would be better for me to die than to live."

God again asked Jonah, "Do you have a right to be angry about the vine?"

Jonah replied, "I do. I am angry enough to die."

That was Jonah's final word to God, as far as we know. The story ends with God saying, "You have been concerned about this vine, though you did not tend it or make it grow. It sprang up overnight and died overnight. But Nineveh has more than a hundred and twenty thousand people who cannot tell their right hand from their left, and many cattle as well. Should I not be concerned about that great city?" (Jonah 4:10).

The Bible gives no reply from Jonah. We have no indication that Jonah had any further ministry. God apparently could not use Jonah until he had a change of heart, as well as a submitted will. And Jonah refused to yield.

This story of Jonah is not limited to history, of course. It's a story that happens again and again. Just recently I heard about a man whom God called to preach. He had an excellent job for a large company, and he decided that he would do a little preaching on the side, but he would still keep his high-paying job. He justified the situation by saying that he would use the money he made to fund himself and not require any church to give him a salary. He had only partially yielded his will to God's will.

This man lost his job and then his family. His entire life crumbled around him. He eventually came to the place of saying, "I'll do it your way, God." God restored his family to him. He enrolled in seminary when he was in his forties and then went to preach. Now he has more fulfillment in his life than he has ever had, even though he makes far less money. His wife and children are happy and supportive. According to his own admission, for the first time in his life, his life has *meaning*.

What is your response today toward God? Toward your enemies? Toward situations that don't turn out the way you had planned or desired? God desires to change your will and attitude. Are you willing to let him do so?

THE THREE CALLS OF GOD ON EVERY PERSON'S LIFE

God issues at least three calls to every person. First is the call to salvation—to accept by faith Jesus Christ's shed blood at Calvary as the all-sufficient, substitutionary, atoning death that brings about the forgiveness of sins, and to repent of sin.

The second call is a call to sanctification or separation. This is a call to a life totally committed to God in such a fashion that sin no longer reigns in our lives. This is a call to allow the power of the Holy Spirit living within us to guide our lives and help us resist temptation.

The third call that God issues is a call to service. This call may be to service for him within the home, in the business world, in the mission field, in an area of volunteer service, or to any number of other arenas. God's call to service is always highly personal and very specific to a person's talents, abilities, gifts, and willingness to be used by God.

Some people rebel against the call to salvation. They resist the gospel message. God cannot issue them a call to sanctification or service until they first yield to the call to salvation, so God's move toward them remains an insistent, persistent, unwavering call to salvation. God's efforts in breaking are all aimed at bringing the person to an acceptance of Christ Jesus and a repentance of sin.

Some people rebel against the call to sanctification. They have accepted God's forgiveness and been converted in their spirits, but they refuse to yield to the daily guidance of the Holy Spirit. They want to continue to walk in the ways of the world, rather than in the paths that God desires. They have accepted Jesus as Savior but have not made a decision to follow him completely as their Lord. God cannot issue them a call to supernatural ministry or service until they first yield to this call to sanctification. He moves relentlessly in their lives until they yield to him. All of his efforts toward breaking are aimed at bringing a person to accept the call to sanctification.

Some people resist God's call to service or to supernatural ministry. They hear God say to them, "I want you to do this." They respond, "I know this is what you said, but I think I'll do this first or instead." They justify their choice by saying it is a way of accomplishing the same goal.

One woman I know heard God say to her very clearly, "You are not to work. You're to stay home with your three children and raise them. They may have fewer things, but they will grow up with more love, more joy, more happiness, and more discipline. This is my desire for them and for you."

She said, "Pastor, I rebelled against what God said to me. I wanted a ministry outside the home. I thought if I had a big ministry elsewhere, my children would admire me and want to serve God. I also thought I could win others to Christ by being a witness in the business world. My children have borne the brunt of my rebellion. They are all in junior high or high school now, and my husband and I have seen each of them swayed by their friends to experiment with things that could bring them great harm. I've resigned my job, and I've decided to stay home with them. I can't make up for the lost years, but I'm hoping that I can still have an impact on their lives."

Those who rebel against God's call to specific service never find true satisfaction or a feeling of fulfillment in the lives they choose for themselves. If we learn anything from Jonah, we must learn that Jonah was a man completely without joy. Rebellion brings no happiness—it brings only sorrow, depression, anger, bitterness, and frustration.

Once God calls you to do something, nothing else you offer as a substitute has any value.

God has never said to me, "Would you *like* to do thus and so?" He has never said to me, "Would you *think* about doing this?" He has never once said to me, "Would you *please* do this?" No. God is very direct. He says, "Here's what I want you to do." His direction is very clear, absolute, and unwavering.

THE ROOTS OF REBELLION

Our rebellion against God has several roots.

Pride

The foremost root of rebellion in our lives is pride. Whenever you and I choose to do something our own way and rebel against God's call, we are saying, "I know better than you know, God."

When people resist God's call to salvation, they are saying, "I know better than you, God, about salvation. I know how to be saved apart from Jesus Christ. I know a way to eternal life apart from him."

When people resist God's call to sanctification, they are saying, "I know better than you, God, how to live in this world and still be saved. I know how to make my own decisions and solve my own problems. I know better than you how to define righteousness."

When people resist God's call to service, they are saying, "I know which ministry is right for me. I know how to be effective and to have a meaningful life. I can define my own spiritual destiny."

And in each case, they are wrong. God has provided the way to eternal life: Jesus Christ. Jesus said, "I am the way and the truth and the life" (John 14:6). He didn't say I am *a* way. He said I am *the* way. God has provided not only our way to salvation, but also through the ongoing ministry of the Holy Spirit, our means for sanctification and daily guidance. When we resist God's methods and means and choose our own way, we are in prideful rebellion.

Fear

A second key root of rebellion is fear. Jonah may very well have been afraid to go to Nineveh. The Ninevites were an idolatrous, wicked, vile people. They were treacherous. Jonah may have feared great persecution as a Hebrew walking through the streets of Nineveh talking about the one true God, Jehovah, to a people who were enemies to the Israelites and who believed in many gods. He obviously feared that God would spare the Ninevites. He may even have feared that God would spare the Ninevites to allow them to move against the Israelites to break something in the lives of God's own people.

Pride and fear are the two foremost roots of rebellion in our lives today.

Ask yourself, "*Why* am I resisting what it is that I know God is asking me to do, to give up, or to change?" What is it that you fear? What form is pride taking in your rebellion?

The stronger the forces of pride and fear at work in your life, the greater your tendency to rebel.

Force of Will

Those with a great deal of pride have very strong personalities. They have a forceful will. Generally speaking, they can take a lot of criticism and rejection, do without a lot of loving, and bull-nose their way through a crisis. They have enough self-determination, persistence, and self-confidence that they continue in rebellion no matter how intense the pressure.

Force of Mind

Others are very strong-minded. They are very clever, and they know how to manipulate or weasel their way through situations. They can figure out how to deliver themselves even from God's breaking process. The greater the pressure God applies to their lives, the more they develop their own "Plan B." In spite of everything that God does, they keep moving on, weaving a rather erratic pattern of detour after detour.

Eventually, we each come to the end of our own mental, emotional, and spiritual ability to handle life. That moment may come on our deathbed. It most certainly comes at death.

God's desire is that we face up to our pride and fear and say to him, "I can't figure out life on my own. I can't manipulate my way to genuine joy, hope, and fulfillment. I need you in my life, God. I trust you completely to do for me what is truly meaningful and important."

ATTEMPTING TO DOWNPLAY REBELLION

Nearly all of us, at some time, have attempted to downplay our own rebellion. We find all kinds of ways to justify our decisions.

At times, we blame others for the pressure we are feeling or the brokenness we are experiencing. We say to ourselves, "I wouldn't be in this mess if that person hadn't wronged me. I wouldn't feel this way if that person hadn't caused me to have this trouble."

At times, we blame past or present circumstances. We say, "Well, I grew up this way so this is the only way I know to live and respond. God knows my past, so he knows that I'm going to respond this way."

We keep rationalizing, running, and rebelling. In fact, when people continually justifies themselves and blame others, that's a sure sign that they are resisting brokenness and are in rebellion.

I know a woman who went to a Christian counselor for several sessions, and every time the counselor said to her, "Here's what the Word of God says," she'd look at the passage in the Scriptures and then come up with a series of "But, but, buts." She finally refused to see the counselor again. She didn't like what he had to say because she truly didn't want to hear the truth. She only wanted to tell her own story. That's rebellion in action.

The right response is to confess, "I am in rebellion against God." The sooner we reach that conclusion and face up to the reality of our behavior, the sooner we can see resolution of our brokenness.

THE HIGH COST OF REBELLION

What did Jonah's rebellion cost him? It cost him the same things it costs us:

Loss of family. Jonah was separated from his people. He bought a ticket, intending to move two thousand miles away from his people. Inevitably, our rebellion will cause us to lose relationships with those we love the most. In choosing to run away to Tarshish, Jonah also experienced a . . .

Loss of job. Whatever career Jonah had, he was apparently willing to abandon it for an unknown life in a foreign land.

Loss of income. With his loss of career, Jonah also lost income. Not only that, but he experienced a . . .

Loss of money or assets. Jonah's ticket to Tarshish no doubt cost him a significant sum. When cargo was being thrown overboard, it is very likely that any worldly possessions that Jonah had brought on board were also lost. Even if they were not thrown over at that point, Jonah lost all his worldly goods when *he* was overthrown.

Not only did Jonah experience material, tangible, and relational loss, but he experienced . . .

A guilty conscience. Jonah knew he was disobeying God.

Estrangement from God. Jonah put himself into a position of being out of fellowship with God.

The entire experience of the storm and being in the fish's belly three days and nights must have been a terrible one. Can you imagine the stench inside a fish's belly? Can you imagine the scramble for oxygen, the slow degeneration a person would feel in his own body?

All of these losses are ones that involve others, but Jonah also experienced great . . .

Emotional bondage. Anger, hatred, and bitterness always create bondage for us. When we hold these emotions toward others, we become a prisoner of our own emotions. Resentment eats away at us. It clouds our vision for the future, dampens our enthusiasm for life, and strips us of joy. Bitterness chokes off our ability to love and receive love. Anger and hatred blot out our faith. Jonah was a man who was in great emotional turmoil. His attitude ate away at his heart just as the worm ate away at the vine that God had provided for shade. It caused him to wither as a human being.

Although we don't know anything about Jonah's family, we can assume that they suffered, too, as the result of Jonah's rebellion. The families and loved ones of those who rebel always suffer to some extent.

None of us can rebel against God without paying an awesome price. If we continue in our rebellion, God eventually says to us, "All right. You win, but you lose." God will shelve us in the very state we have chosen for ourselves.

If we have chosen not to accept God's call to salvation, we remain shelved in that state—unsaved, lost.

If we have chosen not to accept God's call to sanctification, we remain shelved in that area—continually struggling against temptation and the consequences of poor choices, bad decisions, and sin.

If we have chosen not to accept God's call to service, we remain shelved in that area—unfulfilled and struggling to find genuine meaning and purpose for our lives.

Rebellion puts an end to our growth. It robs us of wholeness. It cuts off our ability to mature spiritually.

PRAYING FOR THE PERSON WHO IS IN REBELLION

When we sense that a person is in rebellion, our prayer should be, "God, send that person enough trouble so they will turn to you." This is not a prayer for God to kill the person or utterly destroy them. That isn't what God desires, and it must not be what we desire. But we can pray that God will lead them into circumstances and situations that will break their will and bring them to the point of surrender to him. This is for their ultimate benefit and, therefore, is something good for us to pray.

We do not pray harm on the person's life because we want vengeance or to see the person suffer for something they have done to us. Rather, our prayer that they be broken is a prayer that they be put into a position to receive great blessing!

Once a person is being broken, we must not be too quick to come to their aid, to give solace, or to attempt to remove the pain. In so doing, we are getting in God's way! Our prayer should be, "God, I know that you don't send too much or too little into a person's life. Open their eyes that they might recognize you are at work for their own good. Show me what to do and say so that I might speak the truth to them in love. Guide my actions so I won't get in your way."

I have had a number of people come to me to ask me to pray for them that God might remove certain situations from their lives. This is how the conversation usually goes:

"Do you believe that God knows what is happening in your life?"

"Yes."

"Do you believe God loves you?"

"Yes."

"Then this is what we're going to pray. We're going to pray that you will yield yourself to God so that whatever God is up to, you will allow him to accomplish his purposes. We'll pray that God will uphold and strengthen you so that you will come through this stronger and better and more spiritually mature than before. We're not going to pray for escape, but for God's grace to be at work in your life so that you can face this situation with courage. We're going to pray that you will be able to trust God fully to work this situation for your good."

MISSING OUT ON THE BLESSING

Rebellion, if continued, ultimately causes us to miss out on the blessing God desires for us. It keeps us from receiving the *fullness* of what God has planned for us. We may have a little happiness in life, but we never know the fullness of joy. We may experience a little love in life, but we never know the overwhelming wonder of God's unconditional love. We may have a little hope in life, but we never fully know the hope of glory to which we are called.

Resistance to God keeps us from experiencing the full power, wisdom, and presence of God. It keeps us from blessing. Saying no to God's call on our lives is never worth that price.

Chapter Nine

PREPARATION
TO BEAR
MUCH FRUIT

*W*ho is God? What is your concept of him?

Most people I know will respond readily to this question with these descriptions: Creator, Lord, the Almighty, Heavenly Father. Others may say he is the "Higher Power," "The Man Upstairs," "The Source."

Jesus used very few descriptive phrases in describing God the Father. One of them is found in John 15:1, "I am the true vine, and my Father is the gardener."

In the King James Version this word *gardener* is translated "vinedresser"—the one who tends the vineyard.

Jesus goes on to say this about God the Father:

> He cuts off every branch in me [Jesus] that
> bears no fruit, while every branch that does bear fruit

he prunes so that it will be even more fruitful. You are already clean because of the word I have spoken to you. Remain in me, and I will remain in you. No branch can bear fruit by itself; it must remain in the vine. Neither can you bear fruit unless you remain in me.

I am the vine; you are the branches. If a man remains in me and I in him, he will bear much fruit; apart from me you can do nothing. . . . This is to my Father's glory, that you bear much fruit, showing yourselves to be my disciples. (John 15:2–5, 8)

God prunes us, and he does so for a very specific purpose—that we might come to the place in our lives where we bear much fruit.

This passage echoes what Jesus said in John 12:24, "Unless a kernel of wheat falls to the ground and dies, it remains only a single seed. But if it dies, it produces many seeds." In other words, much fruit.

Fruit in the Scriptures is of two types: inner fruit— qualities of character—and outer fruit—the works that we do that bring glory to God and extend his kingdom.

INNER FRUIT OF THE HOLY SPIRIT

The inner fruit we are to bear is not fruit that we grow. It is fruit produced in us as we remain faithful to the Lord Jesus, or, as Jesus said, as we abide in the vine. The closer we walk with the Lord, moment by moment relying upon the power of the Holy Spirit to work in and through our lives, the more we develop this fruit. We can't acquire it in any other way than to walk closely with the Lord, obeying his guidance and direction on a daily basis.

The fruit is, therefore, *his* fruit. Paul expresses this clearly in Galatians 5:22–23 when he says, "The fruit of the Spirit is love, joy, peace, patience, kindness, goodness, faithfulness, gentleness and self-control."

Brokenness is the pruning process that God uses in order to produce inner fruit—his very likeness.

His Work in Us

Many of us desire for God to do things *for* us. Our prayers are filled with requests that God be Johnny-on-the-spot to meet our needs *right now!* Much of the theology we hear today is self-centered and self-seeking. "God, I want you to heal me. God, prosper me. God, bless me. God, protect me. God, do this, this, this, and this for me."

God is at the center of the universe; we are not. He requires that we serve him. He is not our errand boy. He is the Lord God Almighty. We are highly presumptuous when we demand that he do our bidding. The proper relationship with God is one in which we put ourselves into a position to do *his* bidding.

To be sure, God is our life. We have no life—on this earth or in eternity—without him. Jesus said that he came to give us life and to give it to us abundantly. Our life flows from God, but his life flowing in us includes his character and his will.

When we look to God in any other way, we are into idolatry. When we do not seek the presence of God in us as much as we desire the things that we want God to do for us, we are not worshiping God nearly as much as we are worshiping the provision of God. We are worshiping material things.

Giving Up Our Idols

Idolatry can take subtle forms. The last thing we may want to be is idolatrous—only to discover as God breaks us that we have placed too much value on certain possessions or relationships.

I once gave away all my camera equipment. I "pledged" them away first, but then the day came when I physically turned them over to be sold. Now, I love to take photographs. Through the years, I had invested in top-quality cameras and various pieces of photographic equipment. We were experiencing a need in our church, however, that required extra funds. My personal gift involved the one possession that I cherished the most.

This giving was painful. As much as I wanted to make the gift in my mind, the actual giving of the gift—the day I took the cameras down to the camera store and turned them in for cash—was tough. Something in me was broken, however. I experienced a release in my spirit, a "giving up" of the tight hold I had on this valued possession. I quickly could see how God was at work. He not only used my gift to help resolve the need in the church, but he used my gift to resolve a need in *me*. He pried open my tight grasp on this tangible, material substance I held to be so important.

As it turned out, once I had truly "given" my cameras to God and had surrendered myself anew in this area of my life, he dealt in a sovereign way to restore my cameras and equipment to me. One day a couple of months later I answered the door at my home to find a woman standing there with two bags. She asked, "Are you Dr. Stanley?" When I said yes, she set down the bags, turned, and walked away. I opened the bags to find all my camera gear. I called the camera store owner and he said simply, "A person who wishes to remain anonymous purchased your equipment and asked that it be returned to you." In my heart, I knew the cameras and equipment were not only a gift from this anonymous person. They were a gift from God!

I have seen this same principle work in the lives of countless people. When we give up something to which we are clinging and counting as more valuable than our obedience to God, he often gives us something in return that is even far more valuable or beneficial to us. At times, but not always, it is the very thing we gave up. At other times, it is something different but better.

I have seen this happen in relationships. A woman or man will know before God that they must give up a relationship that they value dearly. God has made it clear that they must break off a courtship, that they are not to marry a certain person. They feel great pain. They feel an immense loss of love. But once they have surrendered their will to God's will and truly have given up the person in their hearts, God moves to provide for them a relationship that is far better and more fulfilling than the one they lost.

In the new relationship, God retains first place in the person's life. The right order of love is established. At times, the person whom God restores to them is the very person they gave up. At other times, it is a different person. Sometimes God leads the person to live a single life, but one they find to be very fulfilling. The key is this: The relationship is one that allows for God to be the foremost recipient of love. That is what God desires from brokenness.

In the situation with my cameras, I *could* have given them physically and still not have given them in my heart. I could have pined for them, resented their loss, or been consumed by an eagerness to replace them. That wouldn't have been a true giving of them.

The same holds true for every person who gives up anything of value to them, including relationships. A person can give up the thing he knows God has asked him to give up and still not "give up" that person or thing in his heart. He can pine for the thing or relationship he has lost. He can continue to grieve the loss for years and years. If God has asked you to give up something, give it up! Give it up literally, and give it up in your heart.

God Is Our All in All

Brokenness brings us to the place where we say, "All that matters is God and his presence in my life." At that point we are in submission. We are desiring from God the production of inner fruit in us, not outer fruit that we can show our friends, brag about, or display as status symbols. God's greatest blessings to us are inner blessings, and foremost among them is the blessing of Christlike character.

Very few of us get up every morning and think about God and what he wants to do in and through us. We wake up with a list of things *we* want to do. We awaken thinking about ourselves—our needs, our appointments, our schedule, our agenda, our desires. God's breaking us is aimed at bringing us to the point where we awaken with God's purposes in mind. Our prayer must become, "What is it that you want me to do, say, and be today in order to bring you glory?"

Developing the Character of Christ

The fruit of the Spirit described by Paul is a description of the character of Jesus Christ. He is the One we are becoming like. His character is marked by . . .

Love. Sacrificial love is the hallmark of Christ's character. Love is giving, and then giving more, and then giving still more. Unless we are broken of our self-centered, self-serving, prideful nature, we cannot give this kind of love.

Joy. A person who has not had the death grip of sin broken in his or her life cannot experience true joy. Our salvation produces joy in us. Each time we are broken by God, sin is defeated in our lives, and joy is the outcome. People who are genuinely broken by God know great joy.

People who still seek to do things their own way are in bondage to human frailties, failures, and weaknesses. They are frustrated, envious of others, and in competition. They have no joy; they may have moments of happiness— a superficial emotion—but no deep, spirit-level joy.

Those who have been broken experience the joy of anticipation—the joy of saying, "I can hardly wait to see what God is going to do today." When God is in complete control of our lives, life becomes an adventure!

Peace. Brokenness produces the peace of Christ—a peace pervasive in one's personality. When we submit our lives completely to Christ, we are saying, "God, I'm yours. Do with me what you desire. My life and times are in your hands." This is a position of complete security because God is only going to do in us and for us what is for our eternal best. We are trusting him solely and fully. The result is peace. We don't have to strive anymore. We don't have to forge our own way, create our own success, or be responsible for all the consequences of our work. God is in control. We can rest in his arms.

What a blessing this peace is to us. As Paul wrote to Timothy, "Godliness with contentment is great gain" (1 Timothy 6:6).

Patience. When we compete with others—seeking to achieve our own glory and doing so at the expense of others—then we are not patient with them. Rather, we are "making it happen," the sooner the better. When God breaks us, we realize anew that our timetable and our definition of success are not his timetable or his definition. His ways, purposes, and plans for us are higher than we had ever imagined. When we know that we are his for all eternity, we are much more inclined to wait on God for the *fullness* of what he will give us, and we are much more inclined to trust that he is at work in the lives of others— again, according to his methods and his timetable.

Kindness. When we are in bondage to the desires of the flesh, rather than the desires of the Spirit, we insist on having our own way. We want what we want, when we want it. We steamroll our will over that of other people in our self-centered, pride-motivated quest for what we perceive to be rightfully ours.

Brokenness brings us to the place where we realize we have no rights. All of our rights are turned over to God. Competitiveness is stripped away from us.

To be freed of competitiveness does not mean that we lose our strength. We always are to stand strong in resisting the devil. We are to be bold in prayer and bold in witness. But brokenness brings us to the place where we realize with great awareness what Paul wrote to the Ephesians: "Our struggle is not against flesh and blood, but against the rulers, against the authorities, against the powers of this dark world and against the spiritual forces of evil in the heavenly realms" (Ephesians 6:12).

Paul said that for this struggle we are to be "strong in the Lord and in his mighty power" (Ephesians 6:10). He wrote to the Corinthians, "Be on your guard; stand firm in the faith; be men of courage; be strong" (1 Corinthians 16:13).

When we know with certainty that our battle is not with people, but with the enemy of their souls, the evil one who is the motivator and instigator of their evil toward us, we find it much easier to be kind to other people. We have a capacity to love the sinner, even as we hate the sin and do spiritual battle against the tempter.

Goodness. Brokenness brings us to the place where we know that the only goodness we have in us is because the Holy Spirit lives in us. God alone is good . . . and God is in us and with us. His presence in us gives us the desire to do good works, make good decisions, and come up with good solutions because his very nature is good.

As long as we remain unbroken and unsubmitted to God, we are left to our own human flesh-centered definitions for what is good. Those things that we define as good inevitably disappoint us. A good appearance doesn't always attract. A good mind doesn't always come up with an answer. A good income doesn't always supply all that is needed. A good family heritage doesn't always result in personal success. Only what God defines as good has lasting appeal and benefit.

Goodness is expressed in forgiveness. When we are broken, we no longer demand of others the emotional debt they owe because they have mistreated us. We no longer attempt to manipulate people, control people, or punish people for what they have done or for what we suspect they might do. We don't hold grudges. We are quick to say in our prayer, "This person belongs to you, God. I release this person fully to you. I trust you to work in their life."

The goodness of God compels us to look for the good in others and to do whatever we can to build up others. Goodness prompts us to help those in need, to pray for those who don't know the Lord, and to seek justice on behalf of those who are oppressed.

Whatever Jesus did was good. When we experience the goodness of the Holy Spirit flowing in us, we will do the works that Jesus did, and we will be effective in doing them.

Faithfulness. Until we surrender ourselves fully to God, we are always looking over our shoulders and around the next bend to see what else or whom else might satisfy us, help us, love us, or give to us. We are like the husband or wife who still flirts with every other interesting person who comes along. We are unfaithful in our hearts toward God, the genuine lover of our souls, the one who will never leave us or disappoint us or fail to love us.

Brokenness brings us to the place where we say, "I am truly yours, Lord, and nobody else has a claim on my eternal spirit. You alone are God." That is a position of genuine, unwavering faithfulness.

Just as Jesus never left the Father, not for a moment, so the Holy Spirit produces in us a desire to be with the Father and never to leave him, not for a moment.

Gentleness. As long as we remain unbroken and unsubmitted to God, we are looking to sources other than God to meet our needs. We look to ourselves, and most of us realize very quickly we can't meet all our own needs. Therefore, we turn to other people. We demand that they love us, care for us, provide for us, and meet all of our emotional needs. Eventually, we discover that other people fail us as often as we fail ourselves. They are an unreliable source. Our response is to resent them, to be angry at them, to feel bitterness toward them, or to feel frustrated and disappointed by them. What happens when we have those emotions? We act in very ungentle ways!

We say abusive and unkind things. We deal gruffly with people, rejecting, embarrassing, and ridiculing them in public. We "cut them down" and "cut them off." We are harsh with them.

The underlying reason for our behavior is that we are disappointed that they haven't lived up to our expectations.

The reality is, only Christ Jesus can live up to all our expectations. He is the only one who can truly satisfy all of our desires and meet all of our emotional needs. He alone is the one who can provide everything we need, both in this temporal life and in the life to come.

Brokenness brings us to the place where we are able to be gracious and gentle with others because we recognize that God has been gracious and gentle with us. We can trust others to have their needs met by God, and we can enter into a healthy relationship with other people that builds up rather than drains dry.

Self-control. When we turn total control over to God, he gives us back self-control—that is, his ability to say no to Satan's temptations. We have the capacity to resist evil, a capacity that an unsaved person does not have.

One of the traits that God breaks in us is our voracious greed to satisfy our own longings and desires. He breaks us so we will want what he wants. We discover that God wants us to have what we need and what will bring us joy—very often things that we would never have dreamed would satisfy the deepest longings of our heart. Brokenness changes our desires.

THE OUTER FRUIT OF GOD'S INNER PRESENCE

Many Christians believe that the "outer fruit" they are to display are what we might call "church works." They define the Christian life as attending church regularly, reading the Bible, praying, inviting people to church, and belonging to various committees, commissions, and councils.

Brokenness brings us to the place where we redefine the fruitfulness of our witness. The outer fruit that God calls us to produce is to declare his truth and to meet the needs of those who come across our path. We are to be ready witnesses to his love and power:

> Let them do good, that they be rich in good works, ready to give, willing to share. (1 Timothy 6:18 NKJV)
>
> Always be prepared to give an answer to everyone who asks you to give the reason for the hope that you have. (1 Peter 3:15)

The main purpose of the activities that we call "Christian disciplines"—praying, reading and studying the Bible, attending church regularly—is so that we might *know* what to say when a need arises and be motivated immediately to take action when we see someone who requires our assistance. The heat of a crisis is not the time to prepare one's spirit. The Christian disciplines do not make us Christians—rather, they prepare us for the true Christian life, which is a life led by the Holy Spirit daily into specific acts of service that build up the body of Christ and are a strong witness to the unbelievers who watch our lives.

Certainly the Lord calls us to specific supernatural ministries, as we discussed in a previous chapter. God has given us gifts and prepared us for avenues of service. How we act and the decisions we make on a daily basis within those areas of ministry, however, are to be subject to the power of the Holy Spirit's guidance and direction. We are to be totally reliant upon him to set our daily agendas and to govern our daily schedules.

Again, the reason for brokenness is so that we might realize that the life we live is no longer *our* life. It is Jesus' life. We must surrender on a daily basis to the life that he desires to live through us.

What we discover through brokenness is that when we truly submit our will to his will and allow him to work through us, our service to others has much greater power and effectiveness. Indeed, we are enabled to bear much fruit the more we allow wild shoots to be pruned away from our lives.

If you know anything about vineyards, you know that vines need to be pruned each year. In the barren days of winter, pruning looks severe, but when the new growth comes in the spring, one can see the full purpose for pruning. Pruned vines bear more fruit. The old, dead, unproductive wood is removed. All of the nourishment that comes up from the roots goes straight into the branches capable of bearing fruit. These branches that remain after pruning even have a name—"fruitwood."

So, too, with the work of the Holy Spirit. As our flaws and sins are pruned from us, we are capable of being and doing so much more than we were capable of being and doing before God's pruning.

For example, a person may be very eloquent and have great inborn abilities, talents, and personality. He or she may have great charisma and poise. But if God is not at the heart of the way in which these natural traits are manifested, they will appear hollow, false, and self-serving. Only when we give the Lord center stage in our lives will our natural abilities truly flourish and be well received. We must be willing to be broken so that we might bear much fruit.

Do you truly desire God's best in your life?

Do you genuinely want what God wants for you?

Do you long to experience the best of God's blessing?

The way to the blessing of a new character—that of the Lord Jesus Christ himself—and of a new power in your personal ministry and service to others is going to be a path that involves brokenness. God has no other plan for us. Brokenness is *his* way to blessing.

Allow God today to do his work in you. Yield to the lessons he is teaching you. Submit your will to his will. And then see what good God has prepared for you!

Chapter Ten

THE PROMISE
OF BLESSING

$\mathcal{W}$hat is a blessing?

So often in our world today "blessing" is defined as "prosperity." While I am convinced that having sufficient finances and being able to pay one's bills is a blessing, a true blessing from God extends far beyond the earning of money, the acquisition of property, or the accumulation of possessions.

Many single men and women define "blessing" as getting married. Parents consider their children to be a blessing. Health, the beauty of nature, and meaningful work are blessings from God.

Even these blessings—as wonderful as they are— fall short of the full definition of blessing.

A blessing from God is a gift that is intended for our eternal benefit or good. A genuine blessing always has an eternal component.

THE BROKENNESS AND BLESSING OF PAUL

The apostle Paul knew what it was to be broken, and he also knew what it was to experience God's blessing —especially to experience the blessing that comes in the wake of a time of brokenness. His life is one of the amazing miracles of the New Testament.

Paul was born Saul of Tarsus. He had a great heritage and a formidable background—raised as a righteous Jew, but with Roman citizenship. In religious zeal, he strongly persecuted the early Christian church, even causing the imprisonment and death of Christians. He was on his way to Damascus to extend that persecution outside the boundaries of Israel when Jesus Christ—speaking and appearing to him in a vision of bright light—confronted Paul. He submitted his life to Christ and received God's forgiveness.

Paul was strong-willed and aggressive. He was determined to get the job done, regardless of cost. When the Lord Jesus Christ saved him, what was he? A jewel in the rough. God began a work of perfection and preparation in Paul's life—a work of brokenness.

Over a period of three years, the Lord led Paul out into Arabia and later back to Damascus. We don't know fully what Paul did during those years. He met with Peter and James in Jerusalem for a period of fifteen days. He also traveled to Syria and Cilicia. Some fourteen years passed before Paul entered an active preaching ministry. He went through fourteen years of being broken, refined, chiseled, and prepared for supernatural ministry (Galatians 1:15–2:1).

Paul said of this time that he received the gospel "by revelation from Jesus Christ" and that God "was pleased to reveal his Son in me so that I might preach him among the Gentiles" (Galatians 1:12, 15–16).

No one had insights, illumination, or inspiration like Paul. Those years of being isolated with God—allowing God to reveal to him the truth of Christ Jesus through the Scriptures and experience—were highly valuable years in his life.

Once Paul embarked on missionary journeys, he knew what it meant to be persecuted harshly. He was harassed by his enemies, beaten many times with both whips and rods. He was jailed often. He was shipwrecked. Wherever he went, the opposition quickly mounted against him. He knew well what it meant to be rejected, suspected, criticized, ridiculed, harassed, and accused.

Perhaps no other human being has gone through as much suffering, pain, and trouble as Paul did in his years of ministry.

These hardships also served as lessons to him. They refined him in further ways. Perhaps the two greatest lessons Paul learned from his times of brokenness were these: his limitations and God's unlimited grace. Those are the most valuable lessons any of us can learn.

The Lesson of Our Limitations

Paul tells us in his own writings that he had learned that he could not live the Christian life in his own strength. In Romans 7:18–25 we read:

I know that nothing good lives in me, that is, in my sinful nature. For I have the desire to do what is good, but I cannot carry it out. For what I do is not the good I want to do; no, the evil I do not want to do— this I keep on doing. Now if I do what I do not want to do, it is no longer I who do it, but it is sin living in me that does it.

So I find this law at work: When I want to do good, evil is right there with me. For in my inner being I delight in God's law; but I see another law at work in the members of my body, waging war against the law of my mind and making me a prisoner of the law of sin at work within my members. What a wretched man I am! Who will rescue me from this body of death? Thanks be to God—through Jesus Christ our Lord!

God desires for each of us that we come to the end of ourselves, recognizing that we aren't capable of succeeding on our own strength, knowledge, or force of personality.

If we don't learn this lesson, we will continue to rely on ourselves—our background and heritage, our education and degrees, our determination and ambition, our commitment and willpower. God breaks us to teach us that we cannot live an abundant life on this earth or an eternal life in heaven without his help.

The Lesson of Unlimited Grace

The second great lesson that Paul learned from his afflictions was the lesson of God's unlimited grace.

In 2 Corinthians 12:7–10 we read this confession of Paul:

To keep me from becoming conceited because of these surpassingly great revelations [which Paul described as an experience in paradise], there was given me a thorn in my flesh, a messenger of Satan, to torment me. Three times I pleaded with the Lord to take it away from me. But he said to me, "My grace is sufficient for you, for my power is made perfect in weakness." Therefore I will boast all the more gladly about my weaknesses, so that Christ's power may rest on me. That is why, for Christ's sake, I delight in weaknesses, in insults, in hardships, in persecutions, in difficulties. For when I am weak, then I am strong.

Paul had learned that when he was at his very weakest, that's when the power of God was released through him in its greatest intensity.

We don't know the precise nature of Paul's thorn in the flesh. We do know that it was painful because the word he uses for "thorn" implies a sharp, jabbing, relentless pain. We do know that it impacted his physical body because it was a thorn "in the flesh." We know that it put him into a position of feeling insufficient and weak.

This thorn in the flesh acted in Paul's life as a tool of brokenness to bring Paul to the place where he no longer pleaded with God to remove this thorn from his life—something he said he had done three times—but rather, he accepted it as God's means to bring him to the *blessing* of knowing that God was sufficient for him, regardless of any outer circumstances.

I have never experienced what I would call a thorn in my flesh, but I have had personal problems that seemed to be relentless. No matter what I said or did, they continued. They were problems that defied all reason, all logic, all normal means of solution. And the more I prayed that the problems be resolved or removed, the more the problems remained.

At the same time, I could look and see that everything in the supernatural ministry to which God had called me was flourishing. Souls were being saved, people were being helped, the gospel was going into places we had never been able to take it before. God was doing his work in spite of—perhaps even because of—the pain I was experiencing in my personal life.

In times when I was in excruciating inner pain and turmoil, people would come to me and say, "Dr. Stanley, we've never heard you preach better. You've never touched my heart as much as you did this morning. God is really using you to change some things in my life that needed to be changed."

I had to come to the position where I said, "This is your work, God. It obviously isn't my work. If my having this great struggle in my life means that you are receiving more glory and that your purposes are being accomplished, then I choose to be thankful for this problem."

This lesson about the unlimited nature of God's grace is very likely a lesson we only learn when we are brought to the absolute limits of our own endurance and ability to experience pain and suffering. God knows precisely how much heat we can take in his process of refining us to perfection.

REFINED BY HEAT

The refining of precious metals—especially silver and gold—begins at low heats. Certain impurities respond quickly to heat, and they rise to the surface of the metal and are skimmed away. The heat is then increased. Other impurities rise to the top of the cauldron of molten metal and are skimmed off. Only under extremely intense heat will the most stubborn of impurities separate from the heavy metals and rise to the top where they can be removed.

So, too, in our lives. The breaking in our lives is by degrees. God breaks us layer by layer, bit by bit. If God moved immediately to the deepest areas of our lives, we couldn't stand it. We'd be so overwhelmed, not only would our wills be broken, but our very spirits would be shattered.

The most deeply embedded things within us are the things that are subject to the greatest amount of brokenness. Only when these deeply-seated, strongly-entrenched weaknesses or flaws in our spirits are removed can we truly say, "I know God's grace is sufficient for *anything*. I have been stripped of what seems to be my very essence, my very will, my very ability to minister, my very life. I know God is sufficient because he has become my essence, my will, my ministry, my life."

There is a wonderful poem I want to share with you about the crucible of God's refining fire that reveals to us his grace.

> *He sat by a fire of sevenfold heat*
> *As he watched by the precious ore*

And closer he bent with a turning gaze
As he heated it more and more.
He knew he had ore that could stand the test
And he wanted the finest gold
To mold as a crown for the king to wear
Set with gems with price untold.
So, he laid our gold in the burning fire
Though we fey would have said, "Nay,"
And he watched as the dross that we said
We had not seen was melted and passed it away.
And the gold grew brighter and yet more bright
But our eyes were filled with tears.
We saw but the fire, not the master's hand
And questioned with anxious fears.
Yet our gold shown out with a richer glow
As it mirrored a form above
That bent o'er the fire, though unseen by us
With the look of ineffable love.
Can we think that it pleases his loving heart
To cause us moments of pain?
No. But he saw through the present cross
The bliss of eternal gain.
So he waited there with a watchful eye
With a love that is strong and sure
And his goal did not suffer a bit more heat
Than was needed to make it pure.

—UNKNOWN

Paul knew the full intensity of God's refining fire in his life. And out of it he gained an understanding of God's unlimited grace.

FIVE GREAT BLESSINGS FROM BROKENNESS

At least five great blessings come from our being broken.

The Blessing of Understanding God Better

Only as we are broken can we truly begin to understand the nature of God. We may say quickly, "Have your way in my life, God." But what is God's way? The Bible tells us, "For my thoughts are not your thoughts, neither are your ways my ways. . . . As the heavens are higher than the earth, so are my ways higher than your ways and my thoughts than your thoughts" (Isaiah 55:8–9).

As we are broken, we understand the absolutes of God—that his commandments are exact, his promises are sure, his methods and timetable are his own, his provision is complete.

We understand more fully the Scriptures. We see patterns of how God works in human lives. We have a deeper understanding of his love. We know more fully what it means to be accepted by God on the basis of nothing in ourselves, but solely because he is a loving Father. We understand more fully the purpose of the cross. We grow in understanding of God's patience and love and kindness and forbearance. We have an experiential understanding of his long-suffering. We know with a growing certainty that he is in control of our lives completely and eternally.

The breaking process always lifts almighty God, the Cross, the grace of God to a higher level in our lives than we had placed it before. We are given a glimpse of God's glory and of his divine nature. We come to a new depth of understanding of all God's many attributes.

There is no end to what we can learn about God. The blessing is an infinite one because God himself is infinite in his goodness, vastness, and everlasting nature.

The Blessing of Understanding Ourselves Better

As we are broken by God, we come to a much deeper understanding of ourselves. We are able to trace the avenues, thought patterns, and trends of our lives—from our childhood all through our growing up years. We have a new understanding of certain experiences in our past and how they affected us, for better or worse. We see our emotional flaws and discover the weaknesses that we have in showing love to others and receiving love from others. We see our dependency and come face-to-face with our limitations and frailties. We see how fear has stifled us and thwarted God's purposes in us.

We also come to know our God-given talents, gifts, and abilities. We see ways in which the Lord has strengthened us, prepared us, and fashioned us. Through periods of brokenness we see how God has dealt with us in tenderness and mercy.

One of the things that we always understand very clearly in times of brokenness is that we are sinners.

Brokenness always involves sin—the sin of pride, the sin of rebellion, as well as other sinful behaviors that God desires to remove from us. When we are broken, we realize that although we may have accepted Christ as our Savior and are saved, we still have the capacity to sin. That brings grief to our hearts.

The breaking process reveals to us that we are being renewed and continually cleansed, strengthened, and refined by God. Sin is being peeled out of our lives, layer after layer.

Some people believe that when they accept Christ as their Savior, they are completely freed not only from their sinful past but also from any sins they might commit in the future. Our salvation deals with our sin nature. It puts us into a "forgiven" relationship with God. But unless we understand that we still have the capacity to sin, we find ourselves very confused, frustrated, and disappointed in ourselves as time goes by. Eventually, we err. That is not the time to think, "I'm not saved" or "There's nothing to salvation." Rather, our sin should compel us to draw even closer to God, asking him to remove that tendency, that trait, that habit in us.

When we are saved, the power of sin over us is broken. Romans 6:14 declares, "Sin shall not be your master." We are freed from the clutches of the enemy. Our master now is God. Paul goes on to say, "You have been set free from sin and have become slaves to righteousness" (Romans 6:18). This means that we continually are seeking out what it means to live in right relationship with God and to do the good works that God has called us to do in the power of the Holy Spirit. Any time we find ourselves in rebellion, our first impulse must be, "Lord, help me. Cleanse this from me. I submit to you."

This understanding comes to us when God breaks us. This great blessing gives us a wonderful freedom—a freedom from the ravages and devastation of sin.

We are freed of guilt. We have a means of releasing guilt and being forgiven instantly.

We are freed of the responsibility of having to "go it alone" in our sin, of struggling against the assault of temptation. God is with us to strengthen us in resisting the devil and his temptations.

We are freed of confusion, a continual wondering if we are right or wrong. The Holy Spirit quickens our own spirits to convict us quickly and insistently of wrongdoing.

What a wonderful blessing it is to recognize that while we still have the capacity to sin, we have been freed by Christ Jesus to denounce sin, be forgiven of it, and have victory over it!

Along with freedom comes peace, an inner quietness, a feeling that the ultimate struggle of life is over. We are securely in God's hands. We don't need to turn to pills or booze to find peace. Once we truly are broken and our lives are in total submission to God, a peace floods our soul that is beyond understanding, beyond explaining (Philippians 4:7).

The Blessing of Increased Compassion for Others

Along with gaining a greater understanding of the nature of God and of ourselves through brokenness, we begin to look at other people differently. We begin to see that others are no worse, and no better, than we are.

We are all sinners at our core. We all are in need of God's grace and the refining power of the Holy Spirit at work in our lives. We all need to change, grow, and develop in certain ways. None of us is without flaws and weakness.

Through brokenness, we come to the place where we can say:

- "Father, you were patient with me. I can be patient with him."
- "Father, you showed kindness and mercy to me. I can extend kindness and mercy to her."
- "Father, you forgave me. I can forgive this one who has hurt me."

Brokenness makes us less critical and judgmental. It also opens us up in new ways to be vessels of God's love toward others.

One of the most wonderful blessings we can know in life is the blessing of helping someone else come to God and then to grow up in God.

The Blessing of a Greater Zest for Life

When we come to the end of ourselves and stand on the brink of God's unlimited, unconditional love, we find that we have a greater appreciation for all of God's gifts to us. Our hearts are renewed with thanksgiving and an awareness of God's goodness extended to us.

Songs take on new meaning; our singing takes on new life. Our interest in life is rekindled. We feel freer to express ourselves creatively. We are more willing to take risks in communicating with others and in being vulnerable emotionally. The hard parts of our souls break up so that we are quicker to laugh with gusto and cry with tenderness. We have a new ability to have fun—good, clean, pure fun.

The Blessing of an Increased Awareness of God's Presence

God is with us always, but brokenness makes us more sensitive to his presence.

So many times in my life I have thought, *God must have deserted me,* only to realize quickly, *No, he's here.* His presence comes often when we least expect it in our brokenness. He comforts us and gives us the assurance that he will never leave us or forsake us.

It is then, in the intimacy of our spirits, that God speaks to us of his great love for us. He tells us how much he values us and desires good for us. He assures us that he is with us and is working in us and through us.

When we feel assured of God's presence with us, we are secure. There's no greater security. God reveals himself to us as our all-sufficiency, our total provision, our ultimate protection. That releases us from fear, pressure, and worry. It produces in us an abiding peace that cannot be described and an unspeakable joy that fills our hearts to overflowing, regardless of the circumstances.

WORTH THE STRUGGLE

God is patient. He sees the end of our brokenness and knows that the blessings he has for us are worth the wait. When we yield to God's purposes in our lives and begin to experience the blessings that come from brokenness, we, too, can say, "I'm thankful for this trial. Praise God it's over, but praise God, he cared enough to refine me in this way. I wouldn't trade the blessing of this experience for anything in the world!"

Do you suppose that Jesus has ever looked back on his crucifixion and said, "I surely wish that hadn't happened"? No, a thousand times no. He knows the full purpose and blessing of his crucifixion, including the glorious blessing of his resurrection.

The same holds true for us. When we look back on our brokenness from the perspective of blessing, we are grateful that God broke us, we are grateful for all the pain that we experienced.

THE PURIFYING WORK OF PAIN

One day several years ago, a phrase kept coming to my mind as I was praying: "The purifying work of pain." I didn't understand what that phrase meant, but I knew God had planted that phrase in my mind and that it was important. About two weeks later, my mother had a stroke, and over the next three months, I watched her die. I thought this was the pain that God had foretold. The loss of my mother was intensely painful for me, but throughout her suffering, God assured me that he was doing a purifying work in her—and in me. A refining process was going on in our lives.

Little did I know that the pain would not end when my mother died. One situation after the next followed until it seems that the hallmark of the last four years in my life has been pain. Yet, when I look back on those months and years, I truly can say, "I know God has purified me in many ways." God has shown me things about myself and has taught me things that have made me a much stronger, wiser, and better person than I was four years ago. He is turning things for *good*.

I can look back and see how God has softened me up, changed my thinking, expanded my compassion for others who are in pain. I wouldn't trade those changes for anything. What may appear to others from the outside to be devastating, appears to me to be providential. Painful experiences that occur in our lives should not be classified as curses. They have the potential to be the means toward blessing, and we are wise to regard them thus.

This doesn't mean that I understand all that has happened. Some things we may not fully understand until eternity. This doesn't mean that I hurt less. But a perspective that God is at work keeps me from anger, bitterness, and hostility. I have taken the approach, "I'm going to emerge from this pain with an even closer relationship to God. I'm going to grow from this. I choose to be better, not bitter."

If we nurse the hurt, we never win. If we are willing to let go of the hurt that others have caused us, then we are in a position to change and develop and become the people God desires that we be.

THE CONDITION FOR BLESSING

God places only one condition on the blessings that he has for us through brokenness: We must be willing to submit to him.

If we are willing to surrender ourselves to him, he leads us to total victory in the aftermath of brokenness. It may take months or years for that victory to be realized or recognized, but victory is assured.

If we balk in our rebellion and refuse to surrender to him, we greatly curtail God's blessing. He has no less desire to bless us, but we have placed a barrier of mistrust and rebellion between ourselves and his outpouring into our lives. The blessings of God ultimately are all wrapped up in the fact that God is in us and with us and that we are in God. When we refuse to yield to God in an area of our lives, we eliminate God from that area. We erect a wall that he will not violate. And in the process, we lessen God's ability to change us and work through us. We know less of God, less of ourselves, have less compassion for others, less zest for living, and less intimacy with God.

GOD CONTINUES TO WORK IN US

The apostle Paul wrote to the Philippians, "Being confident of this, that he who began a good work in you will carry it on to completion until the day of Christ Jesus" (Philippians 1:6).

God does not give up on us. He will continue to work in us, bringing us to one experience of brokenness after the next, until we are made perfect in Christ Jesus.

Friend, that's not likely to happen before your death. None of us in this life, in our fleshly bodies living in a fallen world, is likely to know perfection prior to our being with our heavenly Father in eternity. The good news is that God always has a new way for us to grow. He always is at work in our lives.

We never outgrow our need to be broken in one way or other. Praise God that's so. He loves us so much that he never gives up on us, never loses interest in us, and never rejects us. His desire is to live in spiritual intimacy with us forever.

He asks only that we trust him to be our God, so that we might be his people and bring him glory.

MY PRAYER FOR YOU

$\mathcal{F}$ather, how loving, how tender, how gentle, how gracious, how good, how vast are your methods for bringing us ever closer to you so that we might experience more fully your love and care for us.

We pray today that you will continue to work in us and through us to accomplish your purposes for us.

For those who are lost, wandering, or floundering today without purpose and direction, I pray that they will turn to Jesus Christ and accept him as their Savior, and then trust him as their Lord. I pray they will allow the Holy Spirit to guide them, renew them, and empower them to live godly lives.

Father, for people who are hungering, thirsting, or yearning for a greater intimacy of spirit with you, or for greater effectiveness in their daily walk and work, I pray that you will answer that cry of their spirit. Break them as only you know where and how to break them, and make them whole. Bring them to spiritual maturity so that you might use them for supernatural ministry.

Teach us, Father. Reveal to us how you desire us to change, grow, and develop. Help us to cast away those things that are contrary to your purposes for us. Help us to embrace those things that you call us to be and do.

We desire more of you in our lives—to know you better, to have a deeper relationship with you, and to feel your abiding presence in our lives always.

Break us, dear Father, so that you might mold us into your image and likeness. We trust you today to work in us for our good and your eternal glory.

In Jesus' name. Amen.